Four Dimensions of
Financial Peace of Mind

RETIRE

TO THE

FULLEST

ERIC CHETWOOD, CFP®

WESTBOW
PRESS®
A DIVISION OF THOMAS NELSON
& ZONDERVAN

Copyright © 2022 Eric Chetwood, CFP®.

All rights reserved. No part of this book may be used or reproduced by any means, graphic, electronic, or mechanical, including photocopying, recording, taping or by any information storage retrieval system without the written permission of the author except in the case of brief quotations embodied in critical articles and reviews.

This book is a work of non-fiction. Unless otherwise noted, the author and the publisher make no explicit guarantees as to the accuracy of the information contained in this book and in some cases, names of people and places have been altered to protect their privacy.

WestBow Press books may be ordered through booksellers or by contacting:

WestBow Press
A Division of Thomas Nelson & Zondervan
1663 Liberty Drive
Bloomington, IN 47403
www.westbowpress.com
844-714-3454

Because of the dynamic nature of the Internet, any web addresses or links contained in this book may have changed since publication and may no longer be valid. The views expressed in this work are solely those of the author and do not necessarily reflect the views of the publisher, and the publisher hereby disclaims any responsibility for them.

Any people depicted in stock imagery provided by Getty Images are models, and such images are being used for illustrative purposes only.
Certain stock imagery © Getty Images.

Author photo attribute: Annie Brown, Annie Brown Photography

Scripture quotations marked NIV are taken from The Holy Bible, New International Version®, NIV® Copyright © 1973, 1978, 1984, 2011 by Biblica, Inc.® Used by permission. All rights reserved worldwide.

Scripture quotations marked NASB are taken from The New American Standard Bible®, Copyright © 1960, 1962, 1963, 1968, 1971, 1972, 1973, 1975, 1977, 1995 by The Lockman Foundation. Used by permission.

ISBN: 978-1-6642-7784-7 (sc)
ISBN: 978-1-6642-7783-0 (hc)
ISBN: 978-1-6642-7785-4 (e)

Library of Congress Control Number: 2022916774

Print information available on the last page.

WestBow Press rev. date: 01/19/2023

Any views or opinions expressed in this book are solely those of the author and do not represent those of people, institutions, or organizations that the author may or may not be associated with in professional or personal capacity, unless explicitly stated. The analysis presented in this book is for informational purposes only. Nothing in this book constitutes investment advice or any recommendation with respect to a particular country, sector, industry, security, or portfolio of securities. All information is impersonal and not tailored to the circumstances or investment needs of any specific person. All investing is subject to risk, including the possible loss of your investment. The advice and strategies contained herein may not be suitable for your situation. You should consult with a professional where appropriate. This book contains statements and statistics that have been obtained from sources believed to be reliable but are not guaranteed as to their accuracy or completeness. The past performance of a mutual fund, stock, or investment strategy cannot guarantee its future performance. Diversification does not guarantee investment returns and does not eliminate the risk of loss. The author, along with any of the author's partners or associates, shall not be liable for any loss of profit or any other commercial damages, including but not limited to, special, incidental, consequential or other damages.

"Certified Financial Planner Board of Standards, Inc. (CFP Board) owns the CFP® certification mark, the CERTIFIED FINANCIAL PLANNER™ certification mark, and the CFP® certification mark (with plaque design) logo in the United States, which it authorizes use of by individuals who successfully complete CFP Board's initial and ongoing certification requirements."

Endorsements

"Scripture tells us that the secret to living a meaningful life in the present is thinking about it from the perspective of an eternal future. This book contains more than practical advice on investing and saving, though it contains a lot of that (Eric has been an invaluable counselor to me on these things!). It is an insightful look at whether your investing and saving strategies are moving you toward your deepest life aspirations."

—J.D. Greear,
Pastor of The Summit Church, Durham, N.C.,
Author of *Gospel*

"I know Eric as a great man, humble, serious about his faith, and passionate about his vocation to serve families that want to steward their wealth well. Eric is a great money manager, financial planner, friend, husband, and father…and add to that list, a great writer as well."

—Henry Kaestner,
Former CEO of Bandwidth.com,
Managing Principal of Sovereigns Capital,
and Co-Founder of Faith Driven Entrepreneur

"I enthusiastically recommend 'Retire to the Fullest'! This truly is a 'legacy book' that combines sage financial insights with sound advice on what really matters—both in life and eternity. Thank you, Eric, for the tremendous blessing of this new book. Every page is written from the heart…the heart of a man who knows money, but is also passionate about leaving a lasting legacy!"

—Stu Epperson Jr.,
President of Truth Network
Author of *First Words of Jesus*

Contents

Dedication xi
Acknowledgments xv
Introduction xvii

1 Peace of Mind Begins with a Plan 1
2 Getting to Your Goals 9
3 Constructing Your Investment Portfolio 21
4 Building Wise Portfolios through Diversification 29
5 Chipping Away at Risk 43
6 Behavioral Investing Biases 61
7 Redefining Your Second Half 75
8 The Relational Value of Money 87
9 We All Worship Something 111

Appendix 123
About the Author 129
Endnotes 131

DEDICATION

To the love of my life, Allison. You are such a gift to me and everyone around you. I love you so much.

"Many people retire with a lot of money but very few of them have financial peace of mind."

—Eric Chetwood

ACKNOWLEDGMENTS

To Allison. Thank you for encouraging me and standing faithfully by my side through better or worse, through sickness and health. I couldn't have written this book without your support.

To my favorite boys in the whole world, Noah and James. You are part of the inspiration for this project. It is one of my greatest joys to be your Dad. I love you both more than you could ever understand.

To my friend and mentor, Rick Adams. Many of these lessons I learned from you. Thank you for taking a chance on me and seeing more potential in me than I saw in myself. I owe my career to you.

To Mom and Dad. You both have always been my biggest cheerleaders for as long as I can remember – a rare privilege in today's world that is not lost on me. Thank you for modeling wisdom, grace and truth.

To the many friends that have encouraged me along in this journey that are too many to name –Brett and Jennifer; Brad, Marc, Henry, Stu, JD, Jonathan, Michelle, Katherine, Maria, Audra, the Durham C-12 group, Tim Time guys, and Will. Thank you.

INTRODUCTION

What Is Retirement Anyway?

Her hands were shaking as she reached for her coffee cup. This dear woman had just lost her husband to a sudden and aggressive cancer a few weeks prior. It was my first time meeting her. She was still grieving, but the initial shock of Pete's death had passed. As she spoke a mile a minute, her eyes were dry, but they were filled with something more than tears. They were filled with fear. She was terrified and overwhelmed. Pete had paid all the bills, taken care of all the taxes, and managed all the investments, but now he was gone. She was smart, trained as an ER nurse, but she didn't know where to begin.

Questions came out of her mouth like machine gun bullets: Did she have enough money to cover Pete's medical bills? What were these 1099 forms and K-1s she was getting in the mail, and what should she do with them? Would the IRS come after her if she did the wrong thing? Would she have to sell her house and go live with her sister? She hadn't worked in twenty years because she had raised their kids when Pete got his promotion. Was she going to run out of money? Would she be eating cat food in her old age?

The questions came faster and faster, so I finally took her hand and said, "Marcy. You are going to be fine, and I'll tell you why. Just like you knew what to do when a cardiac patient came into the ER, this is what I do…and I don't mean to brag, but I'm good at what I do. I've helped hundreds of people like you. So, we are going to take a deep breath and not make any big decisions for six months. Over that time, we'll slowly and intentionally put together a wise game plan, and we'll triage appropriately, but I promise you that you will feel much different in one year than you feel right now. In one year, we will have explained what you own, why you own it, what expenses are sustainable, and which ones are not, and when you understand those things, your anxiety will turn into confidence. You are going to be fine, and we will get there together." Marcy took a deep breath, and the fear in her eyes turned into tears—the good kind of tears, and that was when we got to work.

Marcy is part of the reason why I am writing this book. I want to provide a bit of an introduction to explain what I'm trying to accomplish here. It's probably important to say that I've never written a book before. I don't even really consider myself a writer, but I have learned a lot about helping people retire well throughout my eighteen-year career in wealth management, and I am hopeful some of that knowledge will be useful to you.

I started my career in wealth management in 2004, advising and helping clients (like Marcy) on their path through retirement. Along the way, I've learned a great deal about how to help people retire to their fullest, to make the most of not just their money but their lives. This book is my opportunity to share some wisdom with you, wisdom some pay thousands of dollars to get. We'll cover all kinds of topics, including investment strategies, risk management, diversification, stewardship, and so on, but the most important topic on my mind is redefining the meaning and purpose of retirement so you can live a fulfilled, financially peaceful second half of life. There is a path to follow, and it's not a path of enlightenment or a yellow brick road, but it *is* a path that leads to financial peace of mind. Throughout this book, you will hear me say many times that financial planning is so much more than just about finances.

> *"Let's redefine the meaning and purpose of retirement so you can live a fulfilled, financially peaceful second half of life."*

You may be a few years away from retiring and want to make sure you are sufficiently prepared before you pull the trigger. Or maybe you're already retired, but things aren't going the way you hoped. This book will be very helpful to you if you are five to ten years away from retiring or five to ten years into your retirement. That's not to say that someone in their forties will not learn something in these pages, but most of the information is geared around some of the nuances around transitioning from the accumulation phase of life into the distribution phase of life. In other words, it will be *most* valuable to someone approaching that transition from when they draw an income from their paycheck to drawing an income from their nest egg.

Either way, I'm confident you will learn something of value in the following chapters. How can I be so sure? Because the concepts and principles in this book work. These are the same concepts and principles I teach my own clients and put into practice myself. Many of my clients are pre-retirees and retirees who pay a decent amount of money for the lessons I'm going to teach you. My firm manages over a quarter-billion dollars of our clients' hard-earned money, so we've practiced these principles for decades and seen the results firsthand. If you don't glean anything of value, that's okay. You have my permission to throw this book in the trash. Or better yet, donate it to your public library. How about this? If you don't learn anything new in these pages, I'll invite you to Durham, North Carolina, and I'll treat you to a beverage of your choice. I'm easy to find. But if you do learn something new, how about buying an extra copy of the book and giving it to a friend. Sound good?

What Is Retirement, Anyway?

When you think about your ideal retirement, what comes to mind? What will life look like when you're finished working for a paycheck? How will you spend your time? Try to envision it. Are you on a beach? Volunteering at a soup kitchen? Traveling? Playing with your grandchildren? Maybe a bit of all of these things?

Next, who are you doing these things with? Your spouse? Your kids and grandkids? A friend or other family member? Just yourself? Sit in this moment for a little bit and daydream about what the ideal retirement looks like to you. Everyone has their own ideas of what retirement should look like, their own goals, and we'll unpack this more later on.

Now, does your ideal retirement vision change if I tell you that you only have ten years to live beyond your last day of work? What about if you have five years to live? One year to live? It is very important to dream about your retirement in terms of lifestyle and longevity. Why? Because I want you to take steps now that lead you in the direction of your dream. As Andy Stanley says in his book, *Principal of the Path*, "Your direction, not your intention, will determine your destination."[1]

When they think of the term "retirement," many people have a rather fuzzy view of what their future can be like after their working years are over (that is, for a paycheck). I think that's because they don't have a correct understanding of the meaning of the word "retire." My firm has found in our research that the word "retire" literally means to withdraw—to draw back or away from life. I don't want you to withdraw. Instead, I want you to come to the end of your career and engage in a whole new adventure, to enjoy life to the fullest as you begin your second half. In short, I want you to experience every facet of what we call Financial Peace of Mind or FPOM.

The Four Archetypes of Monetary Dysfunction

I have found that many people retire with a lot of money but very few of them have financial peace of mind. It might help you to crystalize in your mind what FPOM is by talking about what it is not. Let me give you a few examples of some people I know who fit this description. Now, these are four of my friends, whose names have been changed to protect their identities. The first of these is a woman named Debbie. Debbie is a wonderful lady and a joy to be around. She lights up the room wherever she goes and has plenty of money. There is statistically no way she can run out of money given her current spending habits, yet every time we see a blip on the market, every time the Dow Jones Industrial Average falls by 200 points, I get a call from Debbie. She is anxious. She is *worried*. She is losing sleep, terrified that she's going to run out of money and she's going to be eating rice and beans, and her kids are going to have to pay her bills. No matter how much I try to console her and show her the statistics behind her financial plan, she is always anxious. Debbie does not have financial peace of mind.

Another friend of mine named David is an incredibly successful attorney. He has a brilliant mind and had a prolific career. He retired a few years ago and now he's just bored. He played golf for a few months. Got

> *"Many people retire with a lot of money but very few of them have financial peace of mind."*

tired of that. Went to the beach and traveled the world for a little while. Got tired of that. Now he has no purpose and no passion. He spends his time watching cable news all day. He actually said to me, "Eric, I feel like after retirement, the only major milestone left for me to accomplish is to die." When he said that, it made me sad for him. So again, plenty of money but no financial peace of mind.

Then there is Steven, who has more money than he knows what to do with. Steven is swimming in money, but he uses it as a means to control and manipulate the people in his life. He's on his fourth marriage. He is estranged from two of his kids. He is stingy. He is alone. It's really heartbreaking because he has everything that money can buy, but he is completely isolated in this world because people don't like being manipulated or bullied by him. He uses money as a means of gaining power over people, and though he is one of the wealthiest men I've ever met, conflict and strife dominate his life. Steven does not have financial peace of mind either.

And finally, meet my friend Brett, who worked in the same job all of his life. He would always say, "I'm just working for the weekend. Another day, another dollar." He didn't enjoy what he did professionally. It was simply a means to an end. He worked in a job he hated for thirty-five years. Now that he has "withdrawn," so-to-speak, he's all about leisure. He wants to go to the beach, and he wants to buy a new boat, and he wants to buy a new car, and he wants to take his wife to Europe, and because he has all this time on his hands, he has developed a bad habit of spending his time spending money. Because he has spent all this money, even though he started out with a very sizable nest egg, his retirement is now in jeopardy. I tie it back to the fact that he worked in a career he hated, so by the time he was set free from that career, he felt like he'd been released from prison. Now it was time to start living, and living for him meant he needed to buy all these toys. While fun for a while, he faces the stress of coming up short. That is clearly not financial peace of mind.

These are actual people I care about, who, I believe, typify the four archetypes of financial dysfunction, representing hundreds of thousands of people just like them who have plenty of money but no financial peace of mind. I believe this book you are reading is a roadmap to help these four friends and the people like them, including you, get to a place of peace in your second half of life.

And while I'm sharing other people's stories to highlight dysfunction, I should probably point the mirror at myself and my own financial dysfunction. My story is another impetus for this book. As I mentioned earlier, I began working in wealth management in 2004. I joined an amazing team and had an absolutely amazing boss who has become a mentor of mine and one of my best friends. In fact, much of this book comes from principles he taught me. His name is Rick Adams, and he deserves a lot of credit for what you're about to read.

Eight years into my job, things were starting to go well for me. I'd worked hard to complete the Certified Financial Planner® coursework over a year. I sat for their ten-hour exam, which by the end of that exam, my brain was so fried I could barely write my name. I was so tired, but I passed the exam and was able to use the CFP® marks, indicating I was now a Certified Financial Planner® and had met the CFP® Board's certification requirements. I agreed to adhere to their high standards of professional competency and ethics, and I was having some success with clients wanting to do business with me.

At that point in time, eight years in, I was asked to become a partner in my firm, which felt really encouraging to me, at least for a while, because shortly thereafter, I had a bit of a crisis of confidence. I kept asking myself and my wife, Allison, "What am I doing with my life? Am I just making rich people richer? Am I making any real difference in the world? Or am I just spending all these hours and days and years on what amounts to nothing?" All of this inner turmoil really bothered me. It felt very empty to me. My life felt frivolous, and I was going into a sort of despair.

I felt the weight of the famous words from King Solomon, the richest man who ever lived, where he says, "Yet when I surveyed all that my hands had done and what I had toiled to achieve, everything was meaningless, a chasing after the wind" (Ecclesiastes 2:11). So if King Solomon felt that way, it's no wonder I would feel that way too. I had an epiphany of sorts as I started coming out of that pit of

> *"Financial peace of mind comes when you understand how money impacts you financially, emotionally, relationally, and even spiritually."*

despair: financial peace of mind is so much more than just financial; it is more than having a lot of money. This idea led me to the thesis of this book, which is to obtain financial peace of mind, you have to understand how money impacts you in four key ways. Sure it impacts you financially, but it also impacts you emotionally, relationally, and even spiritually.

To illustrate, think about a tabletop for a moment. A table's durability and stability is contingent upon the four different legs being healthy and sturdy enough so we can enjoy our table and use it properly. Even one rotting or broken leg creates a wobble, an imbalance, even a collapse. Likewise, if financial peace of mind is our tabletop, the legs of the table would be the financial, emotional, relational, and spiritual components. When all four are healthy and sturdy, we can begin to experience financial peace of mind. The key is identifying how healthy we are in each of these components and making the necessary adjustments so they can produce life within us and not dysfunction.

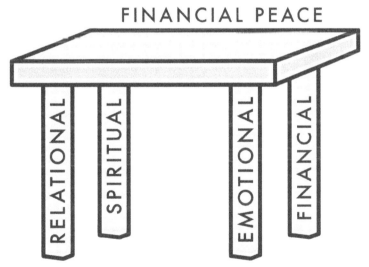

Financial Peace of Mind Tabletop

You may decide that one or more of the dysfunctional archetypes we talked about resonates with you. Maybe you feel deeply entrenched in one of those archetypes or all of them. Be encouraged, my friend. There is hope for you, and all of us, to overcome our shortcomings, our dysfunctions if you will. Half of the battle is realizing we even have them. I think you'll see how each of these four people represent something much bigger, a specific facet of dysfunction, whether that be financial dysfunction, like what we saw with Brett, relational dysfunction, like with Steven, or two different types of emotional dysfunction when we consider Debbie and David.

In the following chapters, we're going to examine each FPOM component in-depth, discussing how to be healthy financially, emotionally, relationally, and spiritually with regards to money, so you can enjoy retirement to the fullest with financial peace of mind.

If all of this sounds intriguing to you, I hope you'll continue with me through the remaining chapters of this book.

Financial Component of FPOM

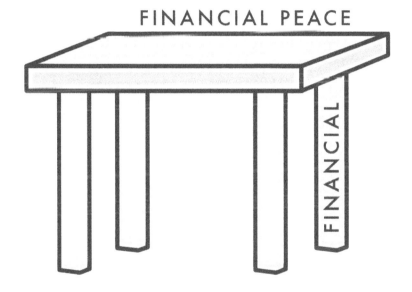

PEACE OF MIND BEGINS WITH A PLAN

We'll begin with the financial dimension of financial peace of mind, the first leg of our FPOM tabletop. This financial component has three parts that build on each other, the first of which is to begin building a *plan* (chapters 1 and 2). Once we have a solid plan, we'll look at how to build an investment *portfolio* that will put us in the optimal position to achieve that plan (chapters 3 and 4). And then, we'll look at any proactive measures we need to minimize various forms of *risk* (chapter 5). If you are extremely confident in the financial leg of your FPOM table, you have my permission to skip over to chapter 6 where we begin our discussion of the second leg, emotional peace of mind. For the rest of you, these next few chapters are what I would consider to be the secret sauce that we've developed over twenty years in our firm - our greatest hits album if you will. Let's get to it.

Imagine a crew of workmen in the mid-1800s clearing a forest full of trees to build a road between two towns. The bulldozer wasn't invented until 1904, so these guys are chopping each tree down by hand, and it is hard work. They've spent weeks chopping and clearing and chopping and clearing until the mayor of the destination town arrives in a huff yelling that they've bypassed the town altogether, which is not good. One of the workmen looks back and notices the road they have been building is curved ever so slightly. Apparently, small curves over a long distance add up to big curves. Tempers flare as the workmen blame each other for making such a foolish mistake. Suddenly, one of the wiser lumberjacks begins climbing one of the trees. His colleagues ask in exasperated tones, "Just where do you think you're going?" He spits on the ground and responds with sage words, "We need to get above the trees to see how to get to where we want to go."

When I interview prospective clients, many of them are so caught up in the chopping and clearing of everyday life that they never take time to get above the trees and see where they want to go and which route is the best to get them there. Is that you? Is it hard for you to take time out of your daily grind to envision your ideal retirement along with the elements of a purposeful second half of life? I'm hopeful that the following pages will help you get above the trees because planning is important. As Benjamin Franklin said, "By failing to plan, you are planning to fail."[2]

> "Financial peace of mind begins with a plan."

So let's start with the plan itself because we thoroughly believe that financial peace of mind begins here. In this chapter and the next, we'll cover the four steps to a good financial plan:

- Articulating your goals—What is important to you?
- Determining key variables of retirement—Can you quantify them as much as possible?
- Taking an inventory of all the assets or resources available to achieve those goals or variables—What is your net worth?
- Stress testing your nest egg's ability to deliver on those goals—Are your goals and ideas even feasible? What adjustments do we need to make to help you get there?

What Matters to You?

When we first meet with a client, our primary objective is to help them define and articulate their goals. Earlier I asked you to envision what your ideal retirement looks like, and that is the first part of our process—to explore that vision, unpack it a little bit, and break it down piece by piece. After that, we write out specific goals within that vision and then quantify those goals and calculate their feasibility. I know you may be thinking, "I don't even know where to start," and that's okay. We all feel that way at first. But not to worry. I help clients build their plans all the time.

To begin building your financial plan, we'll start with three questions, which come from a well-known life planner named George Kinder. They are known as the Three Kinder Questions, which we have summarized for you in appendix 1.[3] The first Kinder question tries to help you figure out your passion in life. Try to imagine that you just won a billion dollars in the lottery. Somehow, you managed to become completely financially secure. Work is now optional. How would you spend the rest of your life? What would you do with your time? And don't hold back. I want you to think about it, to describe in your mind a life that is completely yours. This exercise helps you determine what you are passionate about – what you would do if you didn't need income.

Now assume you get a phone call from your doctor telling you he has some really bad news. You have an incurable illness, and sometime within the next five to ten years, you will abruptly pass away. You're never going to feel sick. You're going to be fully healthy up until the point when you drop dead with no pain. The second Kinder question is what would you do with the five to ten years you have left if you got that phone call? How would your day today change in light of that phone call? These are great questions, aren't they? An old Psalm of Moses says, "Teach us to number our days, that we may gain a heart of wisdom" (Psalm 90:12).[4] There is wisdom in living as though your days are numbered. *What* is important changes. *Who* is important changes. A "numbered-days" mentality forces you to be intentional—to consider the time you have left and live accordingly. So the first Kinder question uncovers passion, the second Kinder question uncovers priority.

And finally, the third Kinder question. Pretend with me for a moment that you get another phone call from your doctor, and he shocks you with the news that they misread the lab results and now you have *one day* left to live. Just sit in that moment for a bit. A sense of mourning starts to creep in as you think through all the things you will now miss out on. Some of you may have received a phone call similar to that on behalf of a family member, and it's really scary. Take just one more moment to feel the weight of that death sentence, and think about which of your dreams will be left unfulfilled. Think about what you wish you had gotten to do or be a part of. By unpacking these desires and going through these mental exercises, it helps you prioritize what really matters to you, allowing you the opportunity to plan around those things.

So what's important to you? What matters to you? Is it more time or intentionality with family? That's a really common response we get when we ask these questions. Is it more experiences with loved ones? "I've always wanted to take my wife to Tuscany" or something like that? Another common response we hear from people is, "I wish I would've made sure that those who are left behind, those I love, are taken care of." Knowing this, what do we need to do today to make those things happen? Do we need to do some estate planning? Have an attorney draw up a will? Do you need to get some life insurance or book a flight to Tuscany? This process is how we help our clients envision their future.

Quantifying the Key Variables of Retirement

Once you have a good, clear picture in your mind's eye for how you want your retirement to go, then we go to work in terms of quantifying every possible variable within that ideal scenario. We thoroughly believe that you can't manage what you don't measure, and that's why we need to quantify these variables. It might look something like this:

"I've always wanted to take my wife to Tuscany."

"Great. How much does it cost to fly from New York to Italy? What does it cost to rent a car or a moped and rent a villa there and eat at the little cafe near the Tower of Pisa?"

If we can quantify the variables there, then and only then can we come up with a plan. So we want to identify specific dreams and put a price tag on them.

Generally, for many people, the first variable that comes to mind is the age you want to retire. And again, I introduced to you earlier the concept that the word "retire" means "to withdraw." So from here on out, instead of using the phrase "I'm going to retire," I want you to use the phrase "I'm going to

> *"Instead of using the phrase 'I'm going to retire,' let's say, 'I'm going to pivot to another passion.'"*

pivot." We're going to pivot to another passion instead of withdrawing. For our purposes, when we talk about what it means to pivot, this is the age when you stop drawing an income from your paycheck and start drawing an income from your investments instead. So what age will that transition, that pivot, happen for you?

The second variable for most people is about what their expenses will be. We think through things like what it will cost you to live when your house is paid for, and the kids are off the payroll. And yes, we generally recommend that before you stop relying on a paycheck and start relying on income from your nest egg—your house is paid off, and your kids are off the payroll.

And then the third variable I want you to think about is the goals you have regarding gifts made to heirs and charity. What do you want your legacy to be? We'll discuss the empirical and academic importance of having charitable goals later on, but for now, do you have specific gifts or requests about what you want to leave your kids or grandkids?

Another variable to think through is, what do you want to spend your time doing? What is your ideal amount of travel? What is your ideal amount of time and money spent on hobbies, golf, ballroom dancing, continuing education, and so on? What are all those things you've always wanted to do, and what does it cost to do them? Sometimes when clients come to us, they'll talk about, "Boy, I've always wanted to have a lake house or a mountain house or a beach house." Great! What does it cost to have that?

We also get questions about how to pay for healthcare or even long-term care in retirement. Many of our clients have had the unfortunate experience of having to navigate a parent through Alzheimer's disease or dementia. They have had a front-row seat to a long-term care situation, and many of them even had to help with the cost of their parents' care. Some of you may not know what necessitates a long-term care situation, so let me pause to give you a brief explanation. If you or your spouse cannot complete two of the five activities of daily living, that is what we refer to as a long-term care situation. Just so you know, the five activities of daily living are bathing, dressing, feeding yourself, toileting, and getting out of bed. So if you or your spouse are ever in a position where you can't do two of these five activities on your own, then you will need to plan for significant costs to have in-home health care or check into a facility. This is definitely something you want to think about well before you need it.

Considering all of these strategic variables is a necessary step when articulating your ideal second half. This is not an exhaustive list of variables but kind of a starter kit to get you on the path of envisioning what retirement looks like and then quantifying the cost. To avoid having you come back to this page hunting for these diagnostic questions later, we've compiled them and more for quick reference in appendix 2.

Now, what if you are a person who doesn't know what your goals are, or you need help thinking through and creating that ideal retirement vision? For starters, that's totally normal. Most people go through life living day to day and "don't have time" to get above the trees. That feeling is understandable, but these questions are really important to think about. I want to encourage you to set aside some time, a weekend or a long afternoon, to get alone with your spouse or significant other, maybe take a walk together to talk about them. Then take some time to marinate on your ideas, which will undoubtedly give you more clarity. Certainly, it could be helpful to meet with a Certified Financial Planner® or a life coach who can facilitate a conversation. By all means, employ people to help you.

Once we know what your goals are, then it's time to figure out how to fund this ideal second half of your life, which starts with knowing how much you are worth financially.

Let's Review

- The first step of building a financial plan is carving out time to get above the trees to envision your ideal retirement. Articulating specific goals is foundational to determining your financial destination.
- If you won $1 billion in the lottery, how would you spend the rest of your life? What would you change about your life today? (Kinder)
- If you were given 5–10 years to live, what would you do in the time you have remaining? (Kinder)
- If you were given twenty-four hours to live, what will you mourn? What will you miss? What will you not get to do? (Kinder)
- Living as though your days are numbered forces you to consider the time you have left and prioritize your goals and life accordingly.
- You can't manage what you don't measure. Once you have articulated the specific goals that comprise your ideal second half, get help quantifying the cost of those goals.

GETTING TO YOUR GOALS

Have you ever seen the iconic Cinderella's Castle at Disney World? You see a replica of it at the introduction of every Disney film. Those introductory clips are strategically placed to transport you and prepare you for a magical experience, and they get me every time. Don't worry, I am not about to make the argument that this next chapter is going to be a magical experience. But I am going to tell you that I've toured the castle that inspired Cinderella's Castle. It is located in Bavaria, Germany, and it was built by King Ludwig II in the late nineteenth century, called Neuschwanstein Castle. If you have never been there, I highly recommend it. It is absolutely breathtaking, and it is relevant to our discussion because the king went bankrupt building his beloved castle, was subsequently deposed, and mysteriously died a few weeks after losing his throne. If Ludwig were here today, he would tell you that a wonderful plan can lead to your ruin if you do not count the cost. You *must* take an inventory of your finances to determine whether your plans will lead to misery or happily ever after. That is what this chapter is about.

Assessing Your Financial Value

Think about when you go to the doctor for the first time. The doctor takes an inventory of every surgery you've ever had, every diagnosis you've ever had, every medication you are currently taking and uses that information to make recommendations to you. In the wealth management industry, we will perform a financial equivalent. Let's start with your net worth.

Now, have you ever seen one of those time-lapsed photos that shows someone before and after they started exercising with the workout de jour? In the first photo, they have a pooch belly, a droopy posture, and they are always very serious for some reason. The last photo shows them smiling radiantly and looking like Adonis. I have never been the subject of such photos, but they are important because they give us a snapshot of a moment in time. We can make deductions about the overall physical health of a person based on those snapshots. Likewise, we can take a financial snapshot to make similar deductions about your financial health. It is called a statement of net worth, the starting point to assess your financial value.

"A net worth statement gives us a snapshot to assess your financial health."

Everyone has a financial value, whether positive or negative. Your net worth tells us what you are worth, in financial terms, at any given moment in time. Calculating your net worth will include taking an inventory of your assets (what you own), as well as any debts or liabilities you may have (what you owe), then subtracting what you owe from what you own. (See appendix 3 for a Sample Net Worth Statement and worksheet.) What you are left with is hopefully a positive number because that is your financial value, which is what we have to work with to make all the dreams you just envisioned into a reality.

To get to your net worth, let's begin by first taking an inventory of your assets, which means everything you own. This is the aggregate value of checking accounts, savings accounts, retirement accounts, other investments, the equity in your home, and the like. To understand all of your assets, we'll ask questions like:

- "What is the value of your house if you were to put it on the market tomorrow?"
- "What's the value of all of your retirement accounts put together, your employer-sponsored retirement accounts like 401(k)s, 403(b)s, TSP accounts, SEP IRAs, Simple IRAs, or individual retirement accounts like Traditional IRAs and Roth IRAs?"
- "What's the value of all of your non-retirement investment accounts? Any other shares of stock that you own? Any CDs or bonds held in taxable accounts?"
- "What is the aggregate value of all the cash you have in checking, savings, money market?"
- "What pensions or other income streams do you have?"
- "What real estate do you have? Does that real estate generate rental income for you, or is it for personal use or vacation use?"
- "Do you own any collectibles, like rare coins, precious metals, rare stamps, or art?"
- "Are you an owner of any closely held businesses, or have you invested in any limited partnerships?"

Once we have those numbers, we'll have a general idea of what you own, so then we can inventory your debts and liabilities, everything you owe. Examples of these might include:

- mortgage
- second mortgage or home equity loan
- home equity lines of credit
- car loans
- credit card debt
- personal loans
- student loans (hopefully, if you are a retiree or close to it, this doesn't apply to you, but maybe you are financing one for a child or grandchild)
- medical debt

We simply subtract your debts and liabilities number from the number that is your assets, and now we know your financial value as a snapshot in a moment in time. Your net worth is the number that is very helpful for us when it comes to different estate planning strategies and how to minimize taxes, which we'll get into later on. Now we can begin testing your nest egg's ability to deliver on your goals, the final part of the planning phase.

Stress-Testing the Nest Egg

I use the word "financial stress test" very intentionally because it is similar to a stress test you may have endured during a physical at a doctor's office. Imagine the doctor hooking you up to a bunch of sensors, then putting you on a treadmill. The goal is to push your body to the brink of what they believe it can handle so the doctor can draw conclusions about sustainability and overall health and wellness.

It's the exact same concept we're talking about here. We believe it is wise to stress-test your nest egg's ability to deliver on your goals, which helps determine the sustainability of your finances and their overall health and wellness. This is where the rubber meets the road. We're basically answering the question, "How much do I need to have saved in order to fund the second half I envisioned when I pivot to another passion?" And for a lot of people, this calculation can take one of three forms.

> *"Stress-testing your nest egg helps determine whether you can deliver on your goals. This is where the rubber meets the road."*

The crudest way to try to project retirement income is to scribble it on the back of a napkin and say, "Well, I'm 65 now. And actuaries expect me to live until age 90, so that's 25 years. And I spend about $100,000 a year." So 100,000 times 25 is $2.5 million." That is the worst of the three ways to figure out the ideal size of your nest egg before pivoting to another passion. I mean, that's better than no plan at all, but it's not much of a plan.

The second method, which is a little more accurate way of projecting retirement income, is searching Google for a retirement calculator to get something called a time value of money calculation (TVM), one of the building blocks of modern finance. You may also see this if you log in to your 401K, and they have a "retirement calculator" for you to use. It is almost always a TVM calculation. The five main variables of that calculation are:

- What is the total present value of all your investments?
- What is the assumed average rate of return on the investments?
- How much time will the money have to grow before you start taking distributions?
- How much will the annual or monthly distribution be?
- How many years will you be taking those distributions (life expectancy)?

Now, the TVM is used in many different fields and professional arenas. Its application is far beyond retirement planning, and while I will say that TVM is better than the back of the napkin calculation, there is a fundamental flaw when using TVM to project retirement income. It needs an average rate of return to work its magic, and average rates of return can be very misleading in retirement planning. For example, let's assume we plug in a 10% average rate of return per year into our internet retirement calculator. Sounds reasonable, right? That is the long-term average of the American stock market. But the market doesn't return 10% year after year after year. It is not a linear process. The market might be up 12% one year, up 27% the next year, and down 7% the following year as it was in 1988–1990.

You might be thinking, "Eric, you idiot, that's why we used the word AVERAGE." Yes, using average rates of returns in the accumulation (pre-pivot) phase of life is fine, but using average rates of return in the distribution (post-pivot) phase of life can be very misleading. There is something called "sequence of returns risk," which is kind of technical, and it wouldn't hurt my feelings a bit if you skipped this section and moved to the next. But if this sort of thing interests you, I will help define the sequence of returns risk by telling you a story.

The chart below demonstrates my point and tells the story of the two families represented in each of the columns. One of those families, we'll call them the Davises, retired with $1 million and ended up living for 20 more years, spending $50,000 from the portfolio per year. The second family, the Johnsons, also retired with $1 million and lived for 20 more years, also spending $50,000 per year. The interesting thing about these two families is that they enjoyed the same *average* rate of return during their retirement but experienced a different sequence for when those returns happened.

Eric Chetwood, CFP®

Sequence of Returns/Volatility Risk
S&P 500 Index Annual Returns

Same data, same average, different order

Year	1989-2008	2008-1989
1	31.69	-37.00
2	-3.11	5.49
3	30.47	15.84
4	7.62	4.91
5	10.08	10.88
6	1.32	28.68
7	37.58	-22.10
8	22.96	-11.88
9	33.36	-9.11
10	28.58	21.04
11	21.04	28.58
12	-9.11	33.36
13	-11.88	22.96
14	-22.10	37.58
15	28.68	1.32
16	10.88	10.08
17	4.91	7.62
18	15.84	30.47
19	5.49	-3.11
20	-37.00	31.69
Average Annual Return	8.43%	8.43%

The index is presented to provide you with an understanding of its historic long-term performance and is not presented to illustrate the performance of any security. Investors cannot directly purchase the index

Retire to the Fullest

Notice I've given twenty years' worth of data from the S&P 500, the most common index in the United States. It represents the performance of the 500 largest companies in America. Looking at a twenty-year period, from 1989 to 2008, you can see the left column represents the Davises experience, as Mr. Davis retired in 1989 and experienced the rates of return chronologically. You'll see in year one that he made 31.69% on his portfolio. In year two, 1990, he lost 3.11% in his portfolio, and so on. The year that Mr. Davis died, he lost 37% of his portfolio in 2008. At the bottom, you see what the average rate of return was on his $1 million throughout that time, 8.43%.

On the other hand, the Johnsons experienced the exact same rates of return, just in opposite order of the Davises. Do you see how the column on the right contains the same numbers as the first column, just in reverse order? Now examine this figure below.

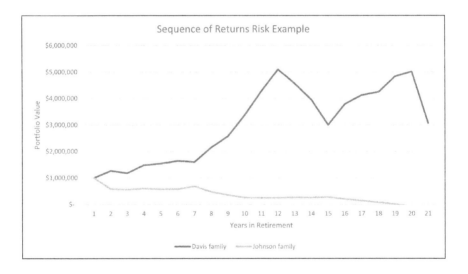

Mr. Johnson (lower line) retired, and in the first year of his retirement, his million-dollar portfolio lost 37%. He's now at $630,000 instead of $1 million, and he is taking out $50,000 on top of that. So at the beginning of year 2, he has $580,000 left to fund the rest of his life's expenses. By taking money out of the nest egg while the market is falling, you'll see that the distributions compound the pain of the 37% market loss, crippling Mr. Johnson's ability to generate the $50,000 he needs for the rest of his retirement. You will see that his portfolio runs out of money in year 19 of 20, whereas Mr. Davis (higher line) was able to enjoy his $50,000 every year and leave his heirs over $3 million. Remember, same average rate of return—wildly different experiences. That, my friends, is sequence of returns risk and why we say average rates of return can be misleading in the distribution phase of life.

While Googling a retirement calculator is better than the back-of-a-napkin approach because it at least uses some foundational financial principles, it can still be very misleading due to the sequence of returns risk.

We need to remember the definition of sequence of returns risk: the risk of taking distributions in a year when the market is falling so that your distributions amplify the portfolio's losses and erode the portfolio's ability to generate sufficient income down the road. All that to say, we need a better means of calculating or projecting retirement income, which is where we're going next. Instead of just using the two possible outcomes, as we did with the Davises and the Johnsons, let's look at a thousand possible outcomes and then run a statistical analysis on those to get a probability of success.

The reproduction of Envestnet | MoneyGuide's worksheet detail, and any other related images, does not constitute an endorsement of any particular firm or individual nor does it indicate that the author(s) have attained a particular level of skill or ability. The content is for illustrative purposes only and is not based on actual client data.

© 2022 Envestnet | MoneyGuide All rights reserved.

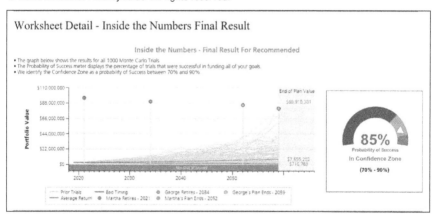

If you look at the table above, you'll see a thousand lines, which represent a multitude of possible outcomes. Compare this to the table before, which only has two lines. When you look at our analysis for George and Martha Washington, there is a little success meter showing an 85% chance that they will be able to retire the way they want to, spend what they want to, and leave behind what they want to. Often, we get the question, "What is a good score when running this type of regression analysis?" An 85% probability of success is the ideal score.

Our office is in Durham, North Carolina, and many of our clients are professors at Duke and UNC. When we show this to them, many of them push back a little bit, saying that an 85% is a B in their class, so how can that be ideal? We always respond by saying that we want to hold two things in tension: you don't want too low of a score because that implies you're living too lavishly and risk running out of money, which is intuitive to people. It's less intuitive to people to not want a 99% probability of success that you can do everything you want, regardless of what happens in the market. If that's true, this implies you're living too frugally, meaning you will end up with a much higher estate legacy than you told us you wanted. If we showed you a 99% probability of success, it would mean that you can easily afford to live more and give more. We're trying to hold those two things in tension.

This analysis is called a Monte Carlo simulation, which is a terrible name, on the one hand, because it gives the connotation of gambling. But actually, if you think about it more, it's a very fitting name because this means of calculation is always focused on calculating probabilities through a myriad of possible outcomes, which is exactly what your retirement plan should be doing. So instead of using the back of a napkin or Googling a TVM calculation by inputting an average rate of return, the Monte Carlo simulation provides much more accurate projections by running a thousand simulations rather than just one or two. Therefore, we apply the principle that we want to measure twice (or, in this case, a thousand times) and cut once.

I realize that some people might be a bit nervous about enlisting the help of a stranger in this process. After all, someone you barely know will be pouring over everything you've spent your entire lifetime building. I can see why this could be a little scary. There are trust issues; I get it! But you would go to a doctor if you found an inexplicable lump in your chest or something like that, right? And when you do, the doctor would ask you all these personal questions. But as the patient, we are willing to disclose the answers because the doctor is probably best equipped to take that information and turn it into something actionable. In the same way, a financial planner is someone highly trained to take the information you give them and confidentially synthesize it to give you an action plan.

Below you will find ten questions that we recommend asking whenever you are interviewing financial planners. They delve into the person and their process, pricing, and practice. You want a financial planner who is objective, competent, transparent, experienced, and honest, but most importantly, you want one who will partner with you through the duration of your lifetime.

Questions to Ask When Interviewing Financial Advisors

People	Process	Price	Practice
How long have you been a financial advisor? Are you a solo practitioner or part of a team? Why?	Are you a fiduciary? Are you required to act in clients' best interest?	How is your compensation structured?	What are your assets under management?
What are your credentials? CFP®? MSF? CKA?	What is your planning process?	What do you do to keep expenses low?	How many clients do you serve and what is their median wealth?
	What is your asset allocation/investment selection process?		How frequently should I expect to review the financial plan together?
			How do you measure client loyalty? What is your NPS score?

By now, you and your financial planner have a good vision for your ideal second half. Once you've quantified any retirement variables, determined your financial net worth, and stress-tested your nest egg's ability to get you where you want to go, then and only then should you talk about the investment strategies you're going to use. And that's where we're headed next.

Let's Review

- Once you've articulated your goals and quantified the cost of those goals, it is helpful to take inventory of the assets you'll use to determine whether those goals are sustainable.
- By subtracting everything you owe (liabilities) from everything you own (assets), you can calculate your financial net worth (appendix 3).
- While better than nothing, simply multiplying the number of years you expect to live by your annual income is not an accurate means of projecting retirement income.
- Using a time value of money calculation to project retirement income can be misleading because of a phenomenon called sequence of returns risk.
- A Monte Carlo simulation is the most accurate means of projecting retirement income because it is based on thousands of simulations rather than an average rate of return.
- Once you have a vision of your ideal second half, and once you've quantified any retirement variables, determined your financial net worth, and stress-tested your nest egg's ability to get you where you want to go, then and only then should you talk about the investment strategies you're going to use.

CONSTRUCTING YOUR INVESTMENT PORTFOLIO

Your investment portfolio should always be constructed as a by-product of the financial plan, not the other way around. Why? Because a seemingly good portfolio may not put you in the best position to get where you want to go. It might have too much market risk built into it or too much inflation risk, which we'll cover later on. By integrating your financial plan with the portfolio, we can establish your ideal retirement as the primary benchmark of success.

Other benchmarks are important as well, such as how the S&P 500 and the MSCI AEFE performed. But we're after financial peace of mind—that is, doing *what* you want to do *when* you want to do it and *not having to worry about money*. This will always be our primary benchmark. Once we have clarity around the statistical feasibility of your ideal retirement, then and only then will we construct the blend of investments that put you in the best statistical position to achieve the goals you've articulated. If we can help you accomplish all the goals you've articulated with as little risk as possible, then we've done our job.

When we're building a portfolio, it's important to understand the tools available to us first. I have many clients who are very intelligent people, with masters and doctorate degrees, and they're otherwise very informed. Yet even the smartest clients get tripped up with the investment vehicles in their portfolio. One of the axioms we talk about all the time is the importance of knowing what you own and why you own it, so let's spend a little bit of time exploring investments tools here.

> *"It's important to know what you own and why you own it."*

Investment Tools

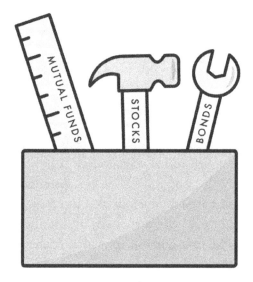

There are really three main investment tools that most investors work with on a regular basis—stocks, bonds, and mutual funds. I'll give you a short explanation of each of these and how they operate mechanically. I really think this explanation will help you understand what you're dealing with when you're building a portfolio or if you're working with a financial planner and allowing them to build a portfolio for you. There are certainly more tools available to you, such as annuities, options, unit investment trusts, hedge funds, real estate, and private equity; but stocks, bonds, and mutual funds are the most common, so we're going to limit our focus to these in this chapter.

Stocks

What is a stock? Warren Buffet always says that when you think about buying stocks in your portfolio, don't think about them as stocks; rather, think about buying ownership into a company.[5] I want you to imagine that you and I are starting a company together building bicycles. We've come up with an amazing new design for a bicycle, and it is the best bicycle in the history of bicycles.

As my partner, the first thing you are going to focus on is the design of the prototype and the building of these bicycles. I'm going to focus on the business and sales aspects of our company. We are both going to contribute a significant but equal amount of startup capital, and we're going to work hard to build this business and split all of the profit 50/50. So then as our bicycle company does well, we both participate in that success commensurate to our ownership in the company. If our bicycle company becomes a billion-dollar business, then you and I, as 50/50 partners, get to split that right down the middle. And the same thing happens if our company goes belly up. We both participate in the pain of that disaster 50/50. We both lose our investment.

So whenever you think about owning shares of your favorite company, such as Amazon, Apple, Procter & Gamble, IBM, and so forth, I want you to understand that you are a fractional owner in that company. Instead of owning it with just one or two other people, you own it with hundreds of thousands of other people, but the concept is still the same. If those companies do very well, you get to participate in their success. If those companies do very poorly, then you will also feel the pain of their failure. So that is what a stock is. It is fractional ownership in a company.

Bonds

Whenever you think about a bond in your portfolio, think of the concept of an IOU. For those of you who are not familiar with IOUs, let me direct you to the 1994 "classic" film "Dumb and Dumber" when the main characters finally return a briefcase that is supposed to be filled with millions of dollars in cash, and instead, it is filled with crumpled little pieces of hand-scribbled paper. The bad guy says, "What is this? Where is all the money?" to which Lloyd, the unemployed imbecile says, "That's as good as money, sir. Those are IOUs. This one is for a car. $275,000 [Lamborghini]. You might want to hang on to that one."[6]

By including that film reference, I've probably destroyed any chance that this book will win a Pulitzer. Still, I think it's helpful to illustrate the vulnerability of IOUs because whenever you buy a bond, like a CD (certificate of deposit), you are lending your money to a bank or a government or a corporation for a period of time in exchange for a fixed interest percentage return. Let's say you give them $10,000, and at the end of five years, they're going to give you your $10,000 back. And for every year, or maybe even twice a year during those five years, they're going to pay you an interest payment for the inconvenience of you not having your $10,000. At the very core of that arrangement is this implicit trust that they will give you your money back. And that's why I think it's so helpful to think of a bond as an IOU, because you may remember your grandmother telling you that a promise is only as good as the person making it.

So if we lend money to an FDIC-insured bank, the trustworthiness of that IOU is considered high because the FDIC, an agency of the federal government, insures it. We know that the probability of getting our money back is relatively high, meaning the risk to us is relatively low. If the risk to us is low, the interest rate on the CD will be relatively low compared to IOUs that might not be as trustworthy. Treasury bonds are also a trustworthy investment since the United States Treasury can always print more currency. If you were to enter into a bond/IOU relationship with them, it's backed by the full faith and credit of the US government, so the interest rate on a US Treasury bond would be lower. High trustworthiness corresponds to safety, which corresponds to lower rates of return.

If the trustworthiness of the borrower is low and the risk is high, then we, as investors, are going to command a higher return. Maybe your Uncle Bruno has told you that he needs to borrow $10,000 from you to start a pizza parlor or a bail bond shop. But Uncle Bruno is not the most trustworthy fellow, and so if you're going to agree to that arrangement, then you're probably going to charge him a much higher interest rate. Lower trustworthiness corresponds to more risk, which corresponds to higher interest rates.

Whenever you think of a bond, think of an IOU. And generally, because bonds promise that you will get every dollar back plus some interest, they are a bit more stable than stocks because they are perceived to have less risk. Stocks generally have a higher ceiling but a lower floor because they typically contain more risk.

Mutual Funds

Finally, let's talk about mutual funds or an exchange-traded fund (ETF), two terms we'll use interchangeably. For this explanation, think back to the time when you were a child, and your favorite food was cereal. I loved cereal as a child, and my favorite brand was Fruit Loops. When my mom would take me to the grocery store, and I wasn't sure whether I wanted Fruit Loops, Corn Pops, or Sugar Smacks, there was this glorious arrangement on the bottom shelf known as the variety pack. And that variety pack gave me instant exposure to many different cereals, which made my decision a lot easier because I could buy the variety pack with all of my favorite cereals bundled together.

The variety pack is a very fitting analogy for what a mutual fund is. If you buy an index fund that tracks the S&P 500, you automatically get fractional ownership in five hundred of the largest companies in the United States. And rather than making five hundred purchases on your own, you can buy one fund and get instant access to all of those companies. That gives you instant diversification, so if one of your companies is the next Enron or the next Wachovia Bank, then you have 499 other companies that are humming along fine.

I think I told you earlier that I began my wealth management career at Wachovia Securities in 2004. I remember when Wachovia was trading at $57 a share and then when it opened at 74¢ a share. What's interesting about that is that Wachovia was known as one of the most conservative banks in the United States at the time. It appeared to many that they could do no wrong due to their conservative underwriting principles, but they made one bad acquisition. They bought a mortgage company out of California in the runup to the Great Recession. And even though that mortgage company represented a very small percentage of their loan portfolio (I think it was less than 4 percent), that one acquisition became cancerous to them. Over several months, they went from $57 a share to 74¢ a share. Imagine if you had all your eggs in that Wachovia basket; the loss would have been devastating. That's why it's valuable to have instant diversification within a mutual fund or an ETF.

So again, think of a mutual fund as a variety pack that allows us to hold many stocks or bonds together, to bundle them and just buy that bundle, rather than having to recreate buying hundreds of individual securities on our own. Doing so allows us to have instant diversification, which reduces risk, a topic we'll discuss in the next chapter.

Another important thing to know when it comes to mutual funds is that there are two primary categories of funds, which we'll look at briefly: Active Funds (Investment Management) and Passive Funds (Index). If you want to buy an index fund that tracks the S&P 500, that is an example of a passive fund. These funds are very inexpensive for investors because they blindly track an index. They're low cost to manage and have very low oversight because as long as they're replicating the index, they're doing their job.

On the other hand, active funds require management by investment companies, who try to select companies within the S&P 500 or any other index that have certain attributes they like. They look for companies they believe have the greatest potential and will lead to the highest return on investment. So active managers buy and sell different companies throughout the year that meet their profile, and they absolutely have a higher amount of oversight. As a result, there will be a slightly higher internal cost with those.

Now there's a lot of academic debate out there about which fund is best for portfolios. Should you use an index fund and just go for the lowest cost, or is there a time when it makes sense to hire an investment manager to add value through active management? Personally, I believe you can use both. We believe that passive index funds represent the best value in some asset classes in the portfolios we manage. And in other asset classes, it makes sense to have an active manager, such as in emerging markets where they don't necessarily abide by our accounting regulations. If an investment manager is thinking about buying a company, they can ask that company, "Hey, how many widgets do you have in inventory?" If that company responds, "We have a hundred thousand widgets," then having a research analyst with boots on the ground who can trust but verify adds value to the shareholder. The investment manager can say, "Hey, I want to go and see the hundred thousand widgets. I'm not going to count every one of them, but don't take me to an empty factory." This added layer of due diligence is valuable, so I feel there are situations where you can use the best of both in terms of active funds or passive funds.

As we conclude our discussion on investment tools, one final theme to keep in mind as we are building portfolios, we want to abide by the words of my business partner, Rick Adams, who said, "We will not be right all of the time, but we do want to be wise all of the time. Because if we're wise all of the time, we'll be right enough of the time." So as that pertains to portfolio management, we try to build portfolios that can stand the test of time and thrive in a variety of different markets. How do we go about doing that? Great question. I'll show you in the next chapter.

> *"We will not be right all of the time, but we do want to be wise all of the time. Because if we're wise all of the time, we'll be right enough of the time."*
> *—Rick Adams*

Let's Review

- Your investment portfolio should always be constructed as a by-product of the financial plan, not the other way around, paving the way for your ideal retirement to be the primary benchmark of success.
- When it comes to investment portfolios, it's important to know what you own and why you own it.
- When you think about owning stocks, think about taking ownership in an actual company. Being an owner allows you to participate financially in the successes and failures of that company.
- Whenever you think about owning a bond, think of an IOU. An IOU is only as valuable as the trustworthiness of the person making it, so different bonds will have different levels of risk and return.
- Generally, less risk corresponds to lower returns, and higher returns require taking more risk.
- Mutual funds are the variety pack of investing. When you buy shares of one mutual fund or ETF, you get instant diversification with access to many different investments at one time.
- When building portfolios, remember that you will not be right all of the time, but you do want to be wise all of the time. If you are wise all of the time, you will be right enough of the time. (Adams)

BUILDING WISE PORTFOLIOS THROUGH DIVERSIFICATION

Just like how you learn letters before you form words and words before you form sentences, you now know the main investment tools we use in portfolio construction. But we still have one more factor to consider—diversification. Most everyone knows that the number-one rule in investing is to buy low and sell high. Right behind that rule is the common phrase, "Don't put all your eggs in one basket." And that concept of not putting all your eggs in one basket is what we call diversification or spreading your risk. I will humbly argue that diversification is the primary mechanism for driving risk-adjusted returns.

So what is diversification, and what is it not? It helps to know that our primary objective for any investment portfolio is to find the right balance between risk and return. A lot of clients say to me, "I want all of the returns from the market, but I don't want any of the downside." They're failing to recognize that risk and return always create a seesaw analogy, where one end of the seesaw is the amount of safety you desire, and the other end is the amount of expected return. If you want more return, you've got to be willing to accept less safety. And if you want more safety, you've got to be willing to accept a lower return. There is always a trade-off.

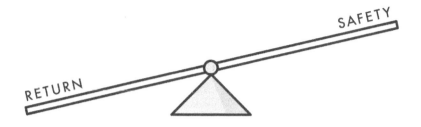

Instead of putting all our eggs in one basket, we diversify, preferring to own many different companies in many different industries of many different sizes, with many different countries represented. We also want them to react differently to the same event. That is critical. By spreading our exposure, we can reduce the impact of any one event, which will lower the overall portfolio risk and provide more consistent rates of return over time.

If you'll pardon the baseball analogy, we explain to clients that we don't want to swing for the fences in our portfolios once they've transitioned to the distribution phase of life (remember sequence of returns risk?). We just want to hit singles and doubles, singles and doubles, singles and doubles. Diversifying is one of the ways we can reduce risk in the hope of generating more consistent rates of return as we continue to hit singles and doubles. This concept of pairing investments that react differently to the same event actually won a guy named Harry Markowitz a Nobel Peace Prize in the early 90s, even though he proposed the concept (called modern portfolio theory) in 1952.[7] So that is diversification.

"Diversifying can reduce risk in the hope of generating more consistent rates of return."

Now, let me tell you what diversification is not. Diversification is not a hodgepodge of mutual funds that duplicate each other. I see this all the time when clients or prospective clients will ask us to review their 401(k) holdings, and they commonly think, "I own eight different mutual funds, so surely I'm diversified." But when you get under

"If everything in your portfolio went up at the same rate over the last year, then by definition, you are not diversified."

the hood of those funds, all eight have Amazon as their largest holding. This scenario was common in the late 90s when everyone loaded up on tech and internet stocks and thought they were diversified. Then in the early 2000s, they found out they really weren't diversified at all. Here's an easy diagnostic tool to see if you are diversified: If everything in your portfolio went up at the same rate over the last year, then by definition, you are not diversified.

Quantifying Diversification

We can quantify diversification by combining what are called non-correlated assets. We need a brief statistics lesson here, so let me define correlation for you because I think that would be helpful to you. Correlation is simply a measure of how two or more variables are related to one another, which is useful when putting together portfolios because correlation can indicate a predictive relationship. There are two types of correlation—positive and negative. I can see your eyes glazing over, but hang with me. This will make sense in three paragraphs.

Positive correlation is when two variables have a direct relationship with one another. I'll give you an example. Recessions and levels of property crime would have a direct relationship with each other, a positive correlation. To the extent we see a recession, we're probably going to have higher property crime levels. The inverse of that would be a negative correlation or an inverse relationship, whereas one goes up, the other goes down. So as the height above sea level goes up, typically you'll find that temperatures go down, and vice versa. If you look at the graph below, it shows how combining negatively correlated assets can really lower the standard deviation of the portfolio or lower the variance of the portfolio, which leads to more consistent rates of return.

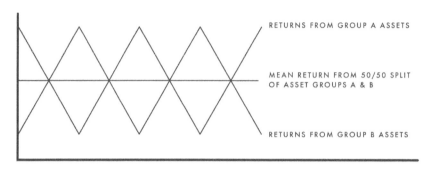

As you can see by the line graph above,[8] we're going to track the performance of investment A. You see that it zigs and zags, and it goes up and down over time. Next to that is investment B, which reacts exactly the opposite. It has an inverse relationship to investment A, so when something happens that causes investment A to go up, investment B goes down, and vice versa. They mirror each other perfectly.

Imagine if the returns of A and B represent a rollercoaster ride. Going up and down and up and down can be very nauseating. What if we put 50% of our portfolio in A and the other 50% in B? Can you see that the combination of the two negatively correlated assets results in a smoother rollercoaster ride? Can you see that it should result in less nausea and more consistent rates of return? Now, this chart is flat from left to right and perfectly symmetrical, which isn't realistic. In real life, there aren't investable assets that have a perfectly negative correlation. But hopefully, you can see the rationale for combining assets that react differently to the same event. As long as A and B are both trending upwards over time, pairing them together can reduce the standard deviation or how violent the rollercoaster ride is for them, which can generate more consistent rates of return for clients. I know this is pretty technical, but truly the information in leveraging non-correlated assets and blending them to smooth out the rates of return in the portfolio not only won Harry Markowitz a Nobel Peace Prize, but it can also absolutely change your life and your retirement.

How to Diversify for Consistent Returns

Once we understand this concept of diversification, what it is and what it is not, and once we are on board with the idea that we're going to use diversified portfolios to generate more consistent rates of return, the question is, how do we apply that practically? Let me introduce you to a concept called *asset allocation*, which is the study of how to apply diversification to determine how much to divide among different investment categories. Because just like our investment A or B, each category, whether it be US large companies or US smaller companies or small international companies or real estate or commodities, each of those categories will have a different level of expected return and risk. In other words, each asset will behave differently over time.

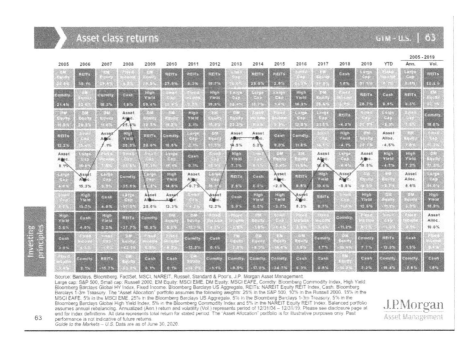

If you look at the chart above, courtesy of our research partners at JP Morgan, you can look at the asset class returns over fifteen years or so. Every year, analysts rank the performance of these different asset classes that are the most common asset classes we use, which I will define for you.

Looking at the earliest column (2005), you see the highest one will be *emerging market equity* (EM equity). Those will be companies domiciled in countries considered to be developing markets or emerging markets. The most common of those will be China, India, Brazil, parts of Latin America, and parts of Southeast Asia. Those can be grouped together a lot of times, and they are referred to as emerging market equities.

The second box below that is *commodities* (Comdty). We usually think of commodities as investments and companies that deal in agriculture, industrial metals, precious metals, and energy, both traditional and renewable.

After that, we see *developed market equity* (DM equity) in the third box. That category consists of countries outside the US that have enjoyed fairly stable, developed economies. The most common will be located in Europe, Japan, Australia, Canada, and countries like that.

The fourth box is REITs, which means *real estate investment trust*. This covers all kinds of real estate, like office buildings, shopping centers, apartment complexes, medical facilities, and so forth.

The box in white below that I will skip over intentionally, as I want to come back to that later.

The sixth box down is *large cap US companies* (Large Cap). Typically, these are companies domiciled in the US that will have an aggregate value or a market cap of greater than $10 billion. Most US companies that are household names fall into this category.

The seventh box is *small cap US companies* (Small Cap), US companies with a market cap or an aggregate value of less than $10 billion. Most of these companies are not yet household names.

The eighth box is *high yield bonds* (High Yield), and remember, when you think about bonds, think of an IOU. When it comes to high yield or junk bonds, think of an IOU issued by a company or an institution whose creditworthiness is somewhat in doubt. Therefore, we will charge a higher interest rate in order to lend them money. That's why they provide a high yield.

Below that in the ninth box is *cash*. I think that needs no explanation.

Fixed income, the tenth box, is debt or bonds issued by companies, governments, or agencies with a higher trustworthiness level—a higher credit rating. They get their own category.

Notice as you go through this chart that it is really hard to see in advance which asset class will be the best performer and which asset class will be the worst performer. That is where we get the theory of a random walk down wall street because it seems so random and hard to predict. I agree that it is hard, if not impossible, to predict which asset classes will be the leaders and which asset classes will be the laggards from one year to the next.

But let's go back to the fifth box, the white box, *asset allocation* (Asset Alloc), which represents a diversified mixture of all these different asset classes that have been put together. You can see that the white box is never the best performer, but it's also never the worst performer. The variance and standard deviation of this white box variety pack have been compressed significantly, leading to more consistent return rates.

And so that study of asset allocation, which asks the question of how much should we allocate to large US companies? 20%? 30%? 40%? How much should we allocate to small international companies? That is the study of how we go about combining those asset classes to optimize the rate of return and the amount of risk we're willing to take to achieve that rate of return. Because again, there's always a trade-off between risk and return.

So here is the culminating question: How do we determine the optimal amount of risk to take that puts you in the best position to achieve your goals? We go back to the stress test. The stress test has already determined the sustainability and viability of your goals, but it can also prescribe the optimal amount of risk/reward trade-off to achieve those goals.

I'll give you three easy examples to show you what I mean. What if we stress-tested your retirement goals assuming a really aggressive portfolio one day, the next day we stress-tested your goals using a really conservative portfolio, and the third day we stress-tested your goals using a 50/50 combination. We would have three different portfolios with three different probabilities of success using the Monte Carlo simulation method that we learned about earlier. Of those three portfolios, would it not be wise to use the portfolio that resulted in the best score after going through the stress test?

Now imagine that we aren't limited to three portfolios—aggressive, conservative, and 50/50. What if we could stress test ten different portfolios or twenty different portfolios with varying combinations of growth and safety? Do you see how we could triangulate down to a portfolio that has the best results in the stress test simulation and how that portfolio represents the optimal mixture of risk and reward? That, my friends, is how we can confidently recommend an allocation that statistically puts you in the best position to achieve your goals—we've run a myriad of data-driven simulations to make sure we get to an optimal blend.

So if we have a seventy-year-old client, and we've stress-tested the viability of his goals across many different portfolios, we could come back with the optimal amount of risk for him to take. We may say, "Mr. Client, we believe that this blend of 60% growth and 40% safety is going to be the best portfolio to get you where you want to go for the long term." And we're not going to follow that allocation over the course of time blindly. We may use our experience or intuition. If we saw a period of time as we did in March 2009, where we think there's so much fear priced into the markets, and valuations of companies are so low that instead of going 60–40, maybe it warrants us being a little bit more growth-oriented. And we might move 10% or 20% to be more growth-oriented.

We may see at the opposite end of the spectrum as we did in the late 90s, where there was so much euphoria about the internet boom. We may say, "Mr. Client, the stress test is recommending that we have 60% positioned for growth and 40% positioned for safety as our equilibrium. However, we are currently seeing valuations that are abnormally high. We think there's a lot of euphoria priced into the market, and therefore, we want to be about 10% even 20% safer than the equilibrium." But we would never say to Mr. Client, "Hey, we've decided that we're going to put 100% of your money in stocks, or gold, or 100% of your money into bonds."

The data-driven asset allocation is always going to be the plumb line with which we build around. And we may flex on that a little bit to the right or the left, but we're always going to have this pressure to come back to the equilibrium. That is how we apply the study of asset allocation. Again, we won't be right all the time. But if we are wise all the time, we will be right enough of the time.

Showing Favoritism for Certain Characteristics

In building our wisest portfolios, we want to acknowledge certain favoritism or bents we have when it comes to investing. So let's discuss these. We will talk a little more about biases in the behavioral investing section of the emotional section later, but I want to discuss the bents or tendencies we condone here.

Minimize Risk

Our primary tendency is to take the least amount of risk to get you to your goals. So in a normal interest rate environment, if we are running a stress test and the 50% growth/50% safety portfolio has the same probability of success within the Monte Carlo simulation as the 70% growth/30% safety portfolio, our tendency is to use the portfolio that has less risk. If you don't need to take that incremental risk to accomplish your goals, it is, by definition, excessive risk, which could jeopardize your ability to reach your goals in some cases, undermining our primary benchmark of success.

Global Bias

Our second tendency is that we like global portfolios. Contrast that to a common error we see, known as home bias, which is the tendency for investors to invest most of their portfolio in companies located in their home country. We see this all the time, and it is understandable because it is familiar to them. But that doesn't make it wise. I'll discuss this more in chapter 6.

Small vs. Large Companies

Our third bent emphasizes smaller companies as opposed to larger companies because, over time, smaller companies have outperformed larger companies for longer stints of time. It is seemingly easier for a $20 billion company to double or triple in size than for a $1 trillion company to double or triple in size.

Value Investing

Our fourth tendency is towards buying companies when they are on sale. Some of you reading this would consider yourselves to be bargain shoppers. My wife is a bargain shopper. She loves to peruse TJ Maxx or Marshalls just so she can find something for a fraction of what her friends paid for it. In the investing world, bargain shoppers are called value investors, which is how I would describe our investing philosophy. It's the same concept. We're trying to buy companies when we believe they are trading at a lower price than their intrinsic value.

Not everyone agrees with this strategy. Some investors are attracted to companies that generate a lot of excitement or hype and trade at a price above their intrinsic value. They rationalize that price because of all the growth that will come when people realize this is the next big thing. We believe it is exceedingly difficult to consistently and accurately predict the next big thing. History is littered with investment opportunities that turned out not to be the next big thing. Do you remember the Palm Pilot? Betamax? Segway? That's not to say we won't own any growth companies, but we prefer to emphasize established, less-exciting companies that have proven a sustainable competitive advantage in their market and buy them when we believe they are in bargain territory. We are guided by the age-old axiom that the cream eventually rises to the top.

Consistent Profitability

Our fifth bent is to buy or emphasize companies that have demonstrated a consistent ability to be profitable. As I mentioned previously, I field many questions about this company or that company that are "sure to be the next big thing." I humbly respond that no matter how great the potential is, it is hard for me to get excited about investing in any company until they can consistently prove they can be profitable. In the chart below, you see companies that have demonstrated profitability have outperformed companies that have not demonstrated profitability. They may have a great idea, but they don't necessarily have a great business yet. As an investor, the difference between those two things is critical to understand.

Overlapping Periods: July 1963–December 2021

HIGH PROFITABILITY beat LOW PROFITABILITY

- 10-Year: 92% of the time
- 5-Year: 81% of the time
- 1-Year: 66% of the time

High is Fama/French US High Profitability Index.
Low is Fama/French US Low Profitability Index.
"There are 583 overlapping 10-year periods, 643 overlapping 5-year periods, and 691 overlapping 1-year periods"

Wide Moat Companies

Our sixth and final bent is toward owning companies that have what Warren Buffett calls "a wide moat," those companies with a sustainable competitive advantage. I'm going to use Coca-Cola as an example of this because when you think about Coca-Cola, it is just sugar and water. Yet we pay a premium to drink their sugar and water. And if you and I wanted to start the next Coke, we would be very challenged to do so because of the high barrier of entry into that industry. We would find it very difficult to replicate the formula of Coke on our own. And even if we did replicate the formula of Coke on our own, we would have a significant branding challenge because the Coke brand is so strong, nobody would know or care about our product.

That concept of owning a company with a wide moat is something we look for. If you think about it, a moat was something used in medieval times where kings would dig a trench around their castle and then put water and crocodiles in that trench to form a deterrent to raiders and enemies who might try to invade the castle. In the same way, companies should be very guarded about their market share.

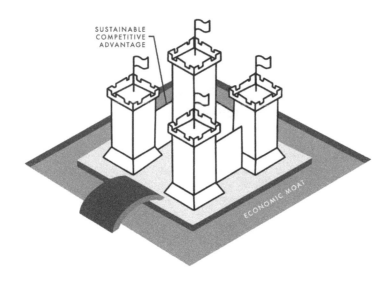

Companies that have a loyal customer base, a high barrier of entry, and can dominate their competition can also command premium pricing. Those companies have what we would call an economic moat or a sustainable competitive advantage. We like these companies because their cash flow is more predictable than their peers, which can translate into more consistent returns for clients.

So far, we've built a comprehensive, stress-tested plan and told you how to build a wise diversified portfolio that integrates with that plan. Now we can turn our focus toward exploring strategies that will help us chip away at various forms of risk that could jeopardize your plan. These risk-mitigation strategies are important because each one will get you closer and closer to financial peace of mind.

Let's Review

- Diversification is the primary mechanism for driving risk-adjusted returns.
- We want to own many different investments from different industries, of different sizes, from different countries, and we want each of them to react differently to the same event. That is diversification.
- If everything in your portfolio went up at the same rate over the last year, then by definition, you are not diversified.
- A Monte Carlo simulation can triangulate your optimal asset allocation, which is the study of how to apply diversification to determine how much to divide among different investment categories.
- Generally, we believe it is wise to take the least amount of risk to get you to your goals. Remember, your ideal retirement is the primary benchmark of success. If you don't need to take that incremental risk to accomplish your goals, it is by definition excessive risk.
- We believe in buying high-quality companies that have a sustainable competitive advantage when they are on sale.

CHIPPING AWAY AT RISK

Let's look at reducing one of the greatest enemies of financial peace of mind—risk. Before we know how to mitigate risk, we have to define it, recognizing there are many different types of risk. Poll a hundred people and ask, "Hey, how would you define risk?" I guarantee you will get many, many different answers. What's risky to you may not be all that risky to me. So for our purposes, we'll define four types of risks that are probably the most common and the most relevant to our conversation.

Four Most Common Financial Risks

Market Risk

When considering financial risk, most people think of something called market risk, which is simply, "I don't want to lose value. I don't want to invest $2 million and then come back three months later and see that I'm down to $1.8 million." The market goes up and down, and when it goes down, it means there are more sellers than buyers. It means the value other investors are willing to pay for our stake in the companies we own is lower than before and vice versa if the market is going up. This is market risk. It's pretty intuitive to people.

Concentration Risk

Concentration risk is defined as any single exposure that can produce losses large enough to jeopardize one's retirement. This is something people intuitively understand is not a smart move to make, yet we see it in practice repeatedly. A client will come to us, having worked in an executive role at the same company for a long time, and we'll find that 30% or 40%, or sometimes even 50% of their liquid net worth is concentrated in the stock of their employer. They don't realize that this is a dangerous risk. Not only is their paycheck tied to the solvency of the company, but a good portion of their nest egg as well. If their employer became insolvent in a short amount of time (which happens more than you'd think), they've lost their livelihood as well as part of their safety net.

Or we'll see that clients just get enamored with a particular company. As we write this book in 2022, Amazon seems like it can strategically do no wrong and dominates every area of the market. Therefore, we understandably have clients who ask us why we are wasting time owning any company other than Amazon in their portfolios. It is human nature, and we'll unpack this a bit more in the next chapter, for people to become enamored with certain companies to the point they build up too big of a concentration in it.

Concentration risk represents a significant risk because I remember a company called Enron. I remember WorldCom. I remember Lehman Brothers. As we said in the last chapter, I remember when Wachovia Bank was one of the most conservative banks on Wall Street, and I remember when they were trading at $57 a share and then fell to 74¢ a share. That didn't necessarily happen overnight, but it happened quickly enough that it jeopardized many peoples' retirements.

Sequence of Returns Risk

We discussed sequence of returns risk in chapter two about how taking withdrawals during a market downturn could erode the nest egg's ability to generate income later on. It's almost like reverse compounding. We talked about how average rates of return can be misleading, particularly in the distribution phase of life. Sequence of returns risk is highly relevant to retirees and a phenomenon that can erode the portfolio very quickly.

Inflation Risk

Finally, inflation—the silent killer nobody talked about until 2022, yet it is completely cancerous to your portfolio. Inflation generally concerns me much more than market volatility. Inflation risk is the notion that the prices of goods and services go up over the course of time, which causes you to lose purchasing power.

I want to share just a quick mathematical trick you can use at cocktail parties to amaze your friends; something called the Rule of 72. The Rule of 72 is very simple. If you take the rate of return in your portfolio and divide that into 72, this will give you the number of years it will take for your portfolio to double at that average rate of return. As it pertains to inflation, if we do the opposite, taking the inflation rate and dividing it into 72, that gives you the number of years your purchasing power will be cut in half.

> *"Taking the inflation rate and dividing it into 72 gives you the number of years your purchasing power will be cut in half."*

So assume you have a $1 million portfolio and the inflation rate goes up to 7.2%, just to make the numbers easy. That would mean we would divide 72 by 7.2, and that would give us ten years for your $1 million to only be able to buy $500,000 worth of goods. That's really scary. For context, the average inflation rate going back to 1950 is about 3.5%. So if we take 72 and divide it by 3.5, then that would mean it would take twenty years for your purchasing power to be cut in half.

So now that we have defined the four most common risks, let's look at how we mitigate each of those so they don't threaten your FPOM.

Eric Chetwood, CFP®

How to Mitigate Financial Risks

Mitigating Market Risk

In the accumulation years, the primary way we mitigate market risk is by having a healthy savings rate. The rule of thumb in the financial planning community is that you want to sock away 15% of your pre-tax income towards your long-term retirement goals in order to continue the lifestyle that you've become accustomed to when you do retire.

At retirement, the distribution phase of life, part of mitigating market risk is making sure you come up with a better way of projecting income or a sustainable spending amount. We know that running a statistical stress test or a thousand Monte Carlo simulations to determine a sustainable spending amount can give us great confidence in a variety of market conditions. Some of those market conditions within the thousand simulations are going to be when the market is cooperative. Some of those simulations will be where the market is anything but cooperative. So, by using the Monte Carlo simulation to calculate your sustainable spending amount and a stress test to optimize your asset allocation, how much growth versus safety, that is a way you can proactively mitigate market risk.

The chart below walks us through some of the factors and variables in retirement. We refer to this as our "control what you can control" chart.

Retire to the Fullest

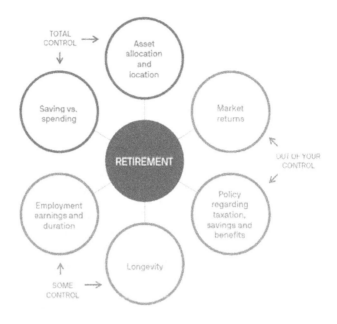

Source: The Importance of Being Earnest, J.P. Morgan Asset Management, 2013

Control what you can control.

The reality is that market rates of returns are not within your scope of control. You don't get to be the arbiter of determining what the market will do next year. If you do somehow have this ability, please let me know as I'd love to bring you on our staff. All joking aside, our strategy of stress-testing some of the worst historical and hypothetical market conditions is our way of applying the old adage to plan for the worst and hope for the best.

As you look again at the chart, you can control your level of spending. You can control your level of saving. You can control how much risk you are taking in your asset allocation and the means of calculation you use. Much is made of election results, and there's a lot of screaming and complaining about tax policy, but other than exercising your right to vote, that's not really within the direct confines of your control. So, you absolutely have control over savings, spending, asset allocation, and means of calculation. You have some control as to how long you work, over the earnings you make during your lifetime, and how long you're going to live based on diet and exercise. So these are relevant to our conversation around market risk.

But you can't control markets. You can only control how you react to the market. That idea is so important that I want you to repeat it with me. Say, "I can't control the market. I can only control how I react to the market." In the next section, we'll talk a little more about the fact that we don't try to time the market because research consistently shows that few have ever been able to time it with consistent success. And by "timing the market," I mean the temptation to jump into the market at just the right time and then jump out of the market and go all to cash at just the right time. That very rarely works, if ever.

"I can't control the market. I can only control how I react to the market."

Mitigating Concentration Risk

How do we mitigate concentration risk? Simple. We use a diversified portfolio. We use a balanced blend of non-correlated assets to build a portfolio that can stand the test of time. Let me tell you a story about a woman named Carol. Carol was a wonderful lady whose husband had worked his entire career at the bank that eventually became Bank of America.

In Carol's million-dollar portfolio, $800,000 of those $1 million were in Bank of America stock. We kept having the conversation, "Carol, I think this is really risky. Empirically, I can show you in our data-driven stress test that this is risky." Carol had sentimental ties to Bank of America because that's what made her think of her husband, who had previously passed away. I always remember her saying that. "Bank of America has always been good to me. They pay a good dividend, and their value has always been stable."

Well, these conversations we were having about concentration risk were happening in the run-up to 2008 when banks' stock prices got slaughtered. Carol passed away in 2006, so it did not impact her, but had she lived longer, her entire retirement would have been jeopardized because of her concentration in one company. Again, I'll point you back to the asset

Retire to the Fullest

class chart that we talked about in chapter four. Diversification drives risk-adjusted returns.

Mitigating Sequence of Returns Risk

How do we mitigate sequence of returns risk? I don't want to beat a dead horse here, but this principle is so important that I'll say it again, and then I'll add a new application to it. We mitigate sequence of returns risk by stress-testing a thousand different simulations so that we don't get caught up in the misleading results of average rates of return, and so we make sure that we get sustainable numbers on our spending and good numbers on our asset allocation. But there is another tool to deploy here, a concept called a *cash flow reserve*. I've included a chart for you because a cash flow reserve will be one of the most intuitive things we talk about. Yet, mathematically, it will have an incredible impact on the longevity of the portfolio.

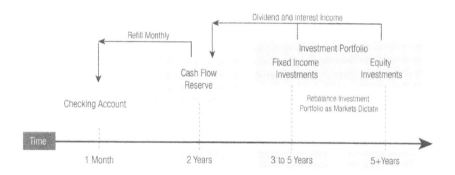

When you think about a cash flow reserve, I want you to think about an agricultural reservoir. Farmers build reservoirs so that if there is a drought, they can still water their crops. Let me give you a financial equivalent to an agricultural reservoir. Before you retire, you're used to receiving a paycheck, and the first line on the chart represents the income that's coming into your checking account. So you may be used to receiving, say, $10,000 a month from your employer. When you retire, some of those income streams may change for you. Rather than getting $10,000 from your employer, you may get $3,000 from Social Security and another $2,000 from your pension. So you'd need to generate $5,000 from your investments.

To do this, we would set up a cash flow reserve that would have a year to two years' worth of the monthly $5,000 need. In this example, we would have $60,000 to $120,000 reserved. There's some give on that depending on how conservative the client is. So $5,000 a month is just going to steadily come from your cash flow reserve into your checking account. That allows us to position the rest of the portfolio so that income generated from dividends and interest can automatically cascade and continually refill the reservoir. Think of it as an income waterfall. Funds continue to cascade and constantly refill that cash flow reserve.

Why is this important? Well, the reservoir serves a few different purposes. First, it puts us in a position where we don't have to sell stocks in a falling market to generate your monthly income. Going back to sequence of returns risk, if the market drops 20%, and I have to sell $5,000 a month to put that into your checking account, I'm selling while the market is falling, and I have to sell more shares to generate your $5,000 a month. That's going to erode the portfolio over time. But if I keep a year or two years' worth of cash as a reservoir, and allow the income to refill that reservoir continually, then I can wait out most of the historical market declines and not sell stocks when the market is falling.

A cash flow reserve provides a second benefit as well. It allows me to put my riskiest assets (think stock funds) on a time horizon where I don't have to touch them for a minimum of five years. That's really important because when we look at historical data, we will find that five years is a magical number. If I can put myself in a position where I don't have to touch my "risky" assets, like stocks, for five years, historically, that dampens the volatility tremendously. Consider the following chart that shows the variance of stock returns going back to 1950.

Retire to the Fullest

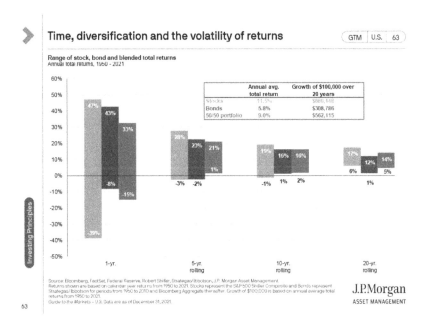

The chart above is also courtesy of JP Morgan, but you will see in the first bar in the grouping to the far left that we can have a lot of variability within stocks in any given year. In any given one-year period, going back to 1950, your return in stocks could be as high as a 47% gain or as low as a 39% loss (hello 2008). If that were a roller coaster, I expect the nausea meter would be high.

But look at the first bar in the grouping that is second from the left. This five-year-rolling-period grouping is what happens if we put ourselves in a position where we're not going to touch this portion of the portfolio for five years. You will see that the variance compresses significantly. That five-year rolling period is historical, again going back to 1950. An example of a five-year rolling period would be 1950 to 1955; 1951 to 1956; 1952 to 1957, all the way to 2020. You will see that if we can just put ourselves in a position where we don't have to touch our risky assets for five years, then we reduce that variance by a significant margin. The worst scenario would be to average a negative 3% rate of return rather than being in a position where we're down 39%. That is quite a difference.

So that reservoir, or cash flow reserve, allows us to put ourselves in a position where we don't have to touch our risky assets (i.e., stocks) for at least five years. If we can do that, we can compress the variance of returns, which leads to more consistent rates of return, which falls into our strategy of repeatedly hitting singles and doubles. Again, it seems very intuitive, but mathematically you'd be amazed at how that one step increases the longevity of the portfolio. We want to put ourselves in a position where we do not have to sell stocks if we see the market drop substantially.

Now, if the market goes up substantially, and we've got a little bit of a shortfall in our cash flow reserve, then, of course, we can use that as an opportunity to take some gains and refill the cash flow reserve. Buy low, sell high, remember? But the critical point is that we don't have to sell anything when the market is falling. Because historically, when we look at big drops in the market, the average amount of time it takes to recover those is generally less than two years. Therefore, if we can just put ourselves in a position where we don't have to sell anything for two years, and we can put all the risky assets so that we don't have to touch them for five years, that drastically helps us mitigate sequence of returns risk. Isn't this fun?

Mitigating Inflation Risk

There are really two ways to mitigate inflation. I'm going to show a chart where stocks have outpaced inflation better than any other asset class.

Over long periods, stocks are our best bet for outpacing inflation. That's why we recommend devoting at least some of the portfolio to owning companies with sustainable competitive advantages. A common question we get is, "If I'm retiring and I want things to be safe, can't I just put everything into bonds or CDs and not have to worry about market volatility?" The answer is you might avoid market risk, but you make yourself vulnerable to inflation risk. Generally, we need some stocks in order to outpace inflation because it doesn't take that long for your purchasing power to be cut in half, as we saw in the Rule of 72 discussion earlier.

In *Simple Wealth, Inevitable Wealth*, Nick Murray made some interesting statements regarding inflation risk (a.k.a. purchasing power risk). He said it really well. Even though most people consider stocks riskier than bonds or cash, you could make the argument that it's riskier to not hold stocks because of the risk of losing purchasing power.[9] Essentially, a diversified mixture of quality stocks are your primary weapon against losing your purchasing power over time due to inflation. Remember what we said earlier, inflation is a silent killer. It doesn't get nearly the headlines that market volatility does, but it is equally pernicious. It is the carbon monoxide of retirement planning, so it is important to consider that when constructing portfolios.

> *"A diversified mixture of quality stocks are your primary weapon against losing your purchasing power over time due to inflation."*

The other way we mitigate inflation risk is by using companies that pay dividends. Now, let me define what a dividend is by going back to the fact that when we own stock shares, we own actual companies. We are fractional owners of the companies we have, and dividends are just a way for those companies to distribute part of their profit to us as owners or shareholders.

To further illustrate, I want you to imagine you are stranded on a deserted island. You have plenty of water but no food. You are scared you will starve to death, and you pray for food. Then out of the heavens, a providential chicken comes flapping madly until it plops down beside you. At that moment, you have a decision to make. You can determine whether you want to make Chicken Marsala for one evening or have omelets for a lifetime. The dividends that companies pay to their shareholders are like the eggs that a chicken lays for the farmer. Dividends are your omelets. We really like the idea of retirees owning companies that pay dividends because you don't have to sell shares, erode your share base, and create capital gains in order to receive income as an owner in those companies. So, dividends are a significant part of our strategy for retirees.

I should delineate a bit further that we like to own companies that are not only dividend payers, but dividend growers. Let me give you an example. In 2020, because of the uncertainty surrounding the COVID-19 pandemic, more than 240 American companies reduced or suspended their dividends.[10] So it's not just enough to say, "I'll just own dividend companies" because not all dividends are created equal. Some are more secure than others. Some companies are heavily reliant on taking out debt to pay those dividends. Therefore, we need to make sure the dividends we are counting on to refill our reservoir are secure.

Furthermore, we like to own companies that have a strong propensity to increase their dividends over time as a way of outpacing inflation. You may have heard of a grouping of companies that are known as "dividend aristocrats" or "dividend kings." These are simply companies that have a long history of not only paying dividends but increasing those dividends. We like to own some of those companies in our portfolios. That's not to say that we exclusively own those types of companies, but we like to emphasize those companies so that clients can have a steady stream of income coming into their checking accounts, which is generally growing over the long term. In our minds, long-term dividend growth will have more of an impact on our clients' financial peace of mind than daily or even weekly price swings within their portfolios.

Now, I feel the need to pause to delineate between a dividend and the dividend yield because many clients conflate the two. They are not the same, and it is important to understand the difference. The dividend yield is helpful to know to compare various companies that all pay different amounts and trade at different amounts. It serves as a ratio that allows you to compare apples to apples. I want you to envision a company with me. As an owner in the company, you get $1 per share each year in the form of a dividend. Let's say it trades at $20 a share. The way we calculate a dividend yield is by taking the income and dividing it by the price. That gives us the yield. So in our example, we have a $1 dividend. Our company is trading at $20 a share. So we divide $1 by $20, and we have a dividend yield of 5%.

Now, imagine something bad happens, and the price of the company falls in half; maybe it goes from $20 a share down to $10 a share. Many people mistakenly think the yield of 5% is what the company has declared. That is not the case. What they have declared is a $1 dividend. So to calculate the updated yield, you divide that $1 dividend by the new price of $10, and you've got a dividend yield of 10%. This is another reason why we like dividend companies. All else being equal, companies who pay dividends will generally not fall as far as those that do not pay dividends. As the price of our hypothetical company falls from $20 to $10, the dividend yield doubles from 5% to 10%. This draws the attention of potential investors to the point that the dividend almost acts as a buoy because there will inevitably be investors who say, "Wow, I can buy in right now at $10 a share. And as long as they don't cut their dividend, I'm going to get an automatic 10% rate of return if the market is flat for the rest of the year, and I'm willing to do that."

So often, we find that dividends buoy the price of stocks during times of volatility, which is another way we can reduce risk and deliver more consistent rates of return to clients. It's important to understand the fundamentals of when a company declares a dividend that they're not declaring the yield. They're committing to a dividend, a fixed payment per share, and we'd divide that dividend by the current price to calculate the yield.

The other benefit of dividend investing is that it allows us to quantify projected income for retirees. We can say, "Ms. Client, this is how much income you should expect to receive in the next year. Even if the market is flat, this is the number of omelets we are projecting, and we shouldn't have to sell shares to generate your $5,000 a month because your chickens are laying eggs."

To summarize how we mitigate inflation risk, we devote some portion of the portfolio to owning quality stocks that generate and grow their dividends. But also, we don't give in to some of the emotional pitfalls that would tempt us to own fewer stocks even though stocks are more volatile. When you consider the impact of inflation on purchasing power over time, you must recognize that market risk and inflation risk is somewhat of a pick-your-poison dilemma and that trade-off is simply a derivative of the trade-off between risk and reward. If you want to combat market risk, you add more bonds. But by adding more bonds, you may make yourself more vulnerable to inflation risk. So, it is critically important to make sure that you have that balance that is not just a feel-good, shoot-from-the-hip kind of balance. It should be a data-driven balance, a statistically-optimized balance.

One final note here. When we talk about dividend yield, it's important to remember that the dividend yield is only part of the total rate of return. Many people will look at the dividend yield on their portfolio statement and assume that is their rate of return. It is not. The rate of return in a portfolio is made up of two components: 1) the income component and 2) the appreciation component. We just explained the income component which can be represented by the yield. The other component of the total rate of return is capital appreciation. For example, if I buy a company at $30 per share and it grows to $40 per share, it has appreciated by $10 or 33%. And so the appreciation percentage plus the dividend yield give us our total rate of return.

In the event that you look at your portfolio and see, "Wow, I'm up 7% thus far this year," you might find that the income generated by the portfolio comprises 2% of your 7%. Logically, that would mean the other 5% of return you received was the appreciation you saw, the prices of the companies you own going up.

We now have all the pieces for the financial component, the financial leg of our FPOM tabletop. For a lot of authors, or financial planners, this is where the story ends. They've given you a lot of formulas. They've given you a lot of definitions, and now you're on your own. However, that is not where we will end our conversation because the three other dimensions are just as important to obtaining financial peace of mind—the next being one of the greatest threats to wealth building and financial peace of mind, the emotional component.

Let's Review

- There are many types of risk; the study of risk is more than just seeing my portfolio go down in value.
- Market risk is the risk of losing money in the ebbs and flows of the market.
- Concentration risk is any single exposure that can produce losses large enough to jeopardize one's retirement.
- Sequence of returns risk refers to taking withdrawals during a market downturn, which can erode the nest egg's ability to generate income later.
- Inflation risk is the erosion of purchasing power over time due to the rise in the cost of everyday living expenses. While not as obvious as market risk, it is equally cancerous to a portfolio.
- I can't control the market. I can only control how I react to the market.
- To proactively mitigate market risk, use a Monte Carlo simulation to calculate the sustainability of your retirement income, as well as the optimal asset allocation.
- Diversification is the primary means of mitigating concentration risk.
- A cash flow reserve puts us in a position where we don't have to sell stocks in a falling market to generate monthly income, which helps mitigate sequence of returns risk.
- A healthy exposure to high-quality stocks with growing dividends is your primary weapon against losing your purchasing power over time due to inflation. In fact, long-term dividend growth will have more of an impact on your financial peace of mind than daily or even weekly price swings within your portfolio.

Emotional Component of FPOM

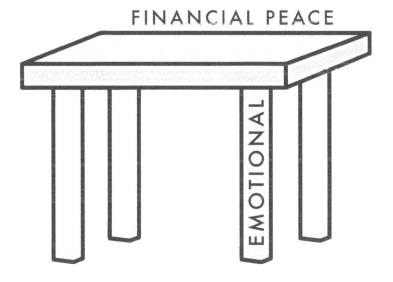

BEHAVIORAL INVESTING BIASES

Have you ever seen someone pursuing a course of action they thought would lead to success, and as an unbiased observer, you knew they were destined for failure? There was a parody video that circulated on YouTube a few years ago entitled "It's Not About The Nail," where a woman complains to her husband about a searing headache that was completely debilitating to her and it's worth your time. "The pain is relentless, and I don't know if it's ever going to stop," she explains. Her husband listens patiently and then says that he thought her headache might be a result of the fact that she had a nail literally sticking out of her forehead. "It's not about the nail!" she says. "Stop trying to fix this." Instead of helping her with the real problem, she wants him to commiserate and feel the pain with her. The video was an instant hit with marriage conferences as they highlighted exaggerated examples of dysfunctional communication. As outsiders, we can see that no amount of commiserating will alleviate this woman's pain until she removes the nail from her forehead.

There is a parallel to this concept in investing. Many people believe that if they can buy the right companies at just the right times, that should be enough to be successful. But I will show you that those two courses of action do not always lead to success. Another factor that is far more important to long-term investing success is your ability to control your emotions.

Consider this quote by Nick Murray in *Simple Wealth, Inevitable Wealth*, where he argues that "Wealth isn't primarily determined by investment performance, but by investor behavior."[11] And that, for a lot of you, is going to be somewhat of a new idea. You'll begin to see the truth of Murray's statement as we introduce this concept of behavioral finance. Behavioral finance is simply the psychological influences and biases that affect investor behavior. It's actually one of the greatest threats to our financial peace of mind.

> *"Wealth isn't primarily determined by investment performance, but by investor behavior."*

Let's go back to my friend, Debbie, the archetype I talked about earlier in the introduction. Debbie is very wealthy. She has plenty of money to live very comfortably, and she can easily accomplish all the goals she has articulated to us. But the problem is, she is anxious and worried much of the time. Every time the market has a blip, she loses sleep, which is not financial peace of mind. Instead of panicking every time the Dow falls 300 points, I want her to rest easy, knowing we developed her plan by anticipating and neutralizing many of the risks she needlessly frets over. Her plan provides her the statistical assurance that she can do everything she says she wants to do.

So right about now, you may be saying, "Well, I'm not like that, Eric. I'm not like Debbie. I have ice in my veins. I don't ever worry about the market." Really? My bet is that you have been tempted by at least one of the behavioral biases I will discuss in this chapter. No one is completely immune to emotional bias when it comes to making investment decisions. It's just human nature. So instead of denying it, it's best to learn about what you might be tempted to do so that you can pursue the wise course of action when the time comes. And remember, we won't be right all the time, but we do want to be wise. And if we're wise all the time, we'll be right enough of the time. Let me share with you six common emotional biases that I see affect clients all the time.

Six Emotional Biases That Affect Investment Behavior

Loss Aversion

This first bias of loss aversion is actually what my friend Debbie suffers from. It is a concept developed by Richard Thaler, which won him a Nobel Peace Prize in 2017. In his book, *Misbehaving*, Thaler concludes that losing money feels twice as bad as making money feels good. And that bias, that feeling of loss aversion, can skew your investment philosophy if you're not careful and affect your investment behavior.[12]

Investors who give in to loss aversion panic when they should sit tight. Imagine you're fulfilling a life-long dream of vacationing in Hawaii. You've dreamt about walking the beautiful beaches and surfing the magnificent waves. You happen to fear flying, so you wear a parachute on board the plane, and for some reason, the airline doesn't stop you. When you inevitably hit routine turbulence over the Pacific, you are feeling really good about your decision to bring your parachute. You prepare to thrust open the cabin door and pull the chord when the pilot tells you that this turbulence is very normal, and pulling your chute over open water will be more detrimental to your health than sitting in your seat and buckling up. While taking action and pulling the ejection handle might feel good to calm your feelings, it is not in your best interest and it certainly will not get you any closer to Hawaii.

Loss aversion bias can tempt people to try to time the market, which is folly. We will discuss this later.

Disposition Bias

Disposition bias is when clients will sell their winners because they like to claim credit for making such a smart investment. "Hey, guess how much I made on company X!" And they'll hang on to their losers because they don't want to admit defeat. I hear all the time, "Boy if I could just get back to even, I'd consider selling it then." There's no comment of, "Well, this is what the growth prospects of this company look like," or "This company is planning to raise their dividend by X percent over the next several years." Instead, there is just this mental anchoring that if I could only get back to the price I bought it for, I won't have to admit I'm wrong.

Eric Chetwood, CFP®

Hear me say this as lovingly as I possibly can. It doesn't matter what a stock did last month or last year, or over the last decade. What matters as an investor is what that company will deliver in terms of growth and profit in the future. The market always looks forward, and you, as an investor, should leave behind mental benchmarks and focus primarily on what the company is going to do from this point forward.

Recency Bias

There is another concept called recency bias, a phenomenon we saw a lot in the Great Recession and the aftermath of 2008. Recency bias takes a small sampling of recent events and extrapolates that trajectory to assume it will lead to a new normal. Typically, this occurs after intense periods of euphoria or depression in the market. 2008 is a great example, where we had many clients who suffered from the old adage "once bitten, twice shy."

In early March of 2009, the S&P 500 traded as low as 666.80 following the financial crisis, and we were adding equity exposure to client portfolios. I kept hearing the phrase, "I would rather wait for the other shoe to drop before I buy." However, we had technically already hit the bottom of the market. And as Warren Buffett always cautions, "They don't ring a bell at the bottom." Conversely, the same is true in periods of euphoria. My business partner, Rick, loves to tell a story of an engineer in 1999, who said, "I think the market has this thing figured out. As we transition to the internet age, computers will be able to value companies more accurately than people will." And even though companies were trading at astronomical multiples of their earnings, he wanted to keep loading up on internet stocks contrary to our recommendation.

The result in 2001 and 2002 for this particular client was disastrous because he got caught up in the euphoria of recency bias. That is why one of the primary ways a good advisor can add value to their clients is to tell them what they need to hear, rather than what they want to hear during times of euphoria and times of depression. A good financial advisor should be an anchor for their clients, not a weathervane.

Home Bias

We touched on the phenomenon of home bias in chapter 4 (Global Bias section), so here is a quick review. Home bias is when investors routinely want to put a higher percentage of their portfolio into companies they are familiar with, usually in the countries in which they live. This could hinder diversification and unknowingly lead to increased concentration risk. Now I'm going to show you two charts, one illustrating the breakdown of the global GDP and comparing it to the other chart that breaks down the global aggregate value as reflected in public stock markets.

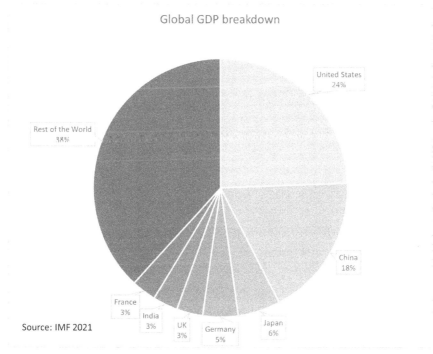

US companies represent 24% of global GDP (production).

Source: MSCI All Country World Index

US companies represent 55% of the global market cap (value).

In the first chart, you'll see that the United States only represents 24% of global GDP (think production). Whereas when we contrast that to the second chart, we will find that American companies represent 55% of the global market cap (think value). So what this means is that even though US companies only produce about a fourth of the goods and services in the world, investors ascribe an aggregate value of more than half of the value of publicly traded companies all over the world, representing an imbalance.

Imagine if you had a sales employee responsible for only generating 25% of your company's sales goals, yet you paid them 50% of total sales bonuses. Wouldn't the rest of the sales team feel a disconnect? Wouldn't the other sales staff start clamoring for bonus size to be commensurate with production? Typically, value is reflective of production.

So why do we see this disconnect when it comes to the US share of global GDP (production) and global market cap (value)? I believe some of that disconnect can be explained by home bias. Citizens of the United States hold huge quantities of wealth compared to the rest of the world, and many US investors choose to invest in what they know.

Why is this a problem? Because over time, in a flat world, where information travels across the globe in nanoseconds, I believe investors will become more familiar with foreign companies. Ultimately, there will be market pressures for value to be reflective of production. US companies that benefit from a familiarity bias but aren't as productive as their foreign competitor will gradually become less attractive. The foreign competitor who demonstrates higher productivity relative to their share price will gradually become more attractive. So why should you care about home bias? Because it is possible that you could have a higher concentration in familiar but less productive companies and find yourself swimming upstream as global values become more reflective of productivity rather than familiarity.

Herd Instinct Bias

Another behavioral bias is the concept of herd instinct, where investors follow what they perceive others are doing or what they see on CNBC or on Fox Business or what their golfing buddies did to make money. Some investors with this bias do what they perceive others are doing rather than relying on their financial plan or their own investment analysis.

The first problem with this practice is that the guy on CNBC may have a financial situation that is very different from yours, and the company he is hawking may be fine, but it might not be the best company *for you*. It might not be the company that will put you in the best position to succeed. The second problem with herd instinct bias is that it usually accompanies the final bias we will discuss next: timing the market.

Timing the Market Bias

Now we get to the most insidious of all emotional biases, which leads clients to want to try to time the market. This bias is probably the most common and the most cancerous bias to your portfolio, so I want to puncture the merit of this luring and prevalent myth.

To do so, we're going to look at something called the Dalbar Study. The Dalbar Group is an analytics firm out of Massachusetts that, since 1990, has published a comparison of returns of different asset classes. For example, they will show the average rate of return of the S&P 500, as well as a lot of other indices, like real estate, gold, commodities, and international equities, over a twenty-year time frame and compare them to what an average investor achieved over the same time frame. You can see in the chart below that over the last twenty years, between 1995 and 2015, the S&P averaged 8.2, whereas the average investor returned 4.7%.

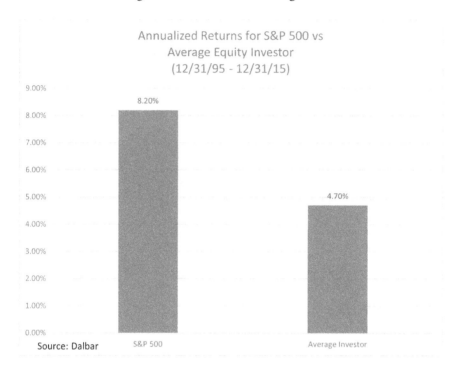

The average investor underperforms compared to the most common indexes.

So what's the reason for such a disparity? Is there a conspiracy that the financial industry is out to get the average do-it-yourself investor? No, it's not. Over many decades, you will find a consistent underperformance of the average investor compared to the most common indexes.

The biggest reason for the disparity? *Investor behavior.* Remember how we said earlier that the number-one rule in investing is to buy when things are low and sell when things are high? Warren Buffett always says, "Be fearful when others are greedy, and be greedy when others are fearful."[13] Even though people know that, even though it is tattooed into their brains, most people don't do that. Let me give you a common scenario.

My friend, Will, is a really smart guy, he recently went to a cocktail party and heard about his friends' investment in a biotech stock. And that biotech firm had gone up in value in a big, big way. So all evening, Will heard his friends talking about how much money they had made in this biotech firm. On his way home from the cocktail party, he starts thinking, "Well, maybe I need to buy some shares of that biotech firm. Maybe I need to add that to my portfolio because that's going to be the next big thing." Sounds like herd instinct bias, doesn't it?

Well, he didn't know about this bias, so he bought. The problem? He bought after a big run-up in the stock price. Is that buying high or low? That's buying high. Well, a couple of months later, we see a routine pullback in the market, and he says to himself, "Oh, I can't take this anymore. I'm going to go to cash because something out of my control, some election, some geopolitical conflict is making me nervous. And so for me to feel better, I'm going to do something about this, and I'm going to sell out of my biotech firm and just put it in cash until I feel better." Watch this, friends. By definition, Will has bought high and sold low. His loss aversion bias just got the best of him, which is why trying to time the market is generally disastrous as an investment strategy. Yet it happens all the time.

We've included a chart below from Carl Richards to help illustrate Will's story, where he buys after a big run-up and sells after a routine downturn.

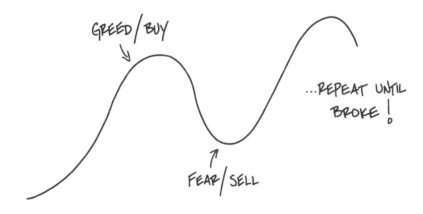

Avoid this behavior!
Source: Carl Richards, www.behaviorgap.com

Here's another example of why timing the market is nearly impossible. Let's talk about the chart below, which compares a $100,000 investment over a 25 year period. The top bar represents someone who stayed invested the entire 25 year period and the subsequent bars show the rate of return had you missed out on the ten best days, twenty best days and so on. Again, we're using the S&P 500 because that's one of the most common benchmarks for the American stock market. We're going to measure the S&P 500 going back to 1997. If you had stayed invested the whole time, your $100,000 would have grown to $1,026,213. If you missed out on the ten best days, your $100,000 investment would have only grown to $470,213.

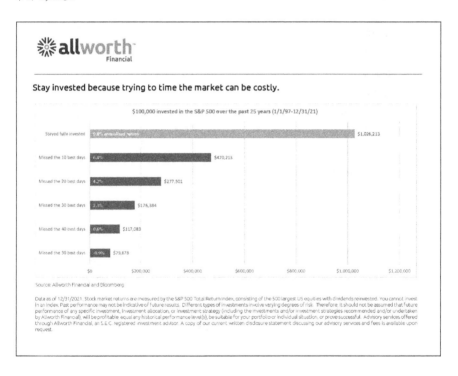

That's a huge difference for just ten days! If we do some quick math here:

Number of years: 25 years

Total possible days of investment: 25 years x 365 days/year = 9,125 possible days

Total days of actual investment if you miss the 10 best days: 9,125 - 10 = 9,115

Percentage of total time actually invested: 9,115/9,125 = 99.89%

Percentage of time not invested: .11%

In other words, you were invested 99.89% of the time, and endured 99.89% of the turbulence but only received less than half the reward. This shows that when you try to time the market, you run the risk of missing out on the ten best days. And I don't know, and you don't know, which days out of the next 9,125 are going to be those ten magical days. And yet, time and time again, people try to time the market. They try to jump in at just the right time and jump out at just the right time.

That's why Peter Lynch, a famous investor who ran the Fidelity Magellan Fund in the 80s and 90s, one of the best in our field, said that far more money has been lost by investors trying to anticipate corrections than has been lost in the corrections themselves.[14]

> *"Far more money has been lost by investors trying to anticipate corrections than has been lost in the corrections themselves."*

So all that to be said, friends, you may think you are completely immune from all of these biases. Maybe you are. Maybe you're not Debbie. Maybe you do have ice in your veins. But maybe you're not. Maybe you have blind spots when you try to invest on your own. That's why we encourage people to at least consider whether they would benefit from a coach or CFP®. If Michael Phelps needs a coach and he's the best swimmer in the world, if Tiger Woods needs a coach and he was the best golfer in the world, maybe you need a coach too. So, again, referring to Nick Murray's *Simple Wealth, Inevitable Wealth*, he gives three ways a coach or a professional advisor might be able to add value to you in light of all of these behavioral biases:

1. A coach or financial planner might be able to increase your return by more than the 1% you would be paying them by creating a portfolio better suited to your long-term goals than the one you'd select if left to your own resources.

2. A financial planner could also save you the equivalent of 1% a year in terms of time and energy and worry that go into managing your investments.
3. The most compelling reason why you should consider using a coach or financial planner is that they may save you some multiple of 1% by coaching you out of making the great behavioral mistakes we just talked about.[15]

Murray goes on to say, "Throwing too much money at an investment fad near its top or panicking completely out of equities near a bottom, to cite just two [behavioral mistakes], cause most investors not merely to underperform the markets, but to underperform their own investments."[16] That's a fascinating quote that you can be invested in a diversified blend of companies, but trying to time the markets would not only cause you to underperform the market as a whole but cause you to underperform the investments that you are in.

So speaking of Tiger Woods. One of the things we encourage clients to think about is that you don't have to be a great investor to have financial peace of mind, but you *do* have to be aware of these behavioral biases. Then you have to *resist* these behavioral biases or have someone in your life who is helping you resist these behavioral biases—somebody who's telling you things aren't as great as they seem, or things aren't as bad as they seem. And that's where we come up with a helpful analogy, also courtesy of Nick Murray: "When you think about scratch golfers or professional golfers, it's not necessarily that they make more amazing shots than the rest of us; it's that they make fewer terrible shots than the rest of us."[17]

We need to tweak our investment philosophy to avoid some of these catastrophic behavioral misses, and a coach can help with that. Once we do that, we'll be well on our way to securing the emotional dimension and achieving FPOM.

We've just covered a big concept in terms of behavioral investing mistakes. I think it might be worthwhile to pivot a little bit and look at a completely different type of emotional dysfunction that threatens financial peace of mind: the idea of a false identity and recovering our true identity, which is the topic of our next chapter.

Let's Review

- A key ingredient to long-term investing success is your ability to control your emotions.
- Wealth isn't primarily determined by investment performance but by investor behavior. (Murray)
- Loss aversion is the emotional bias that recognizes losing money feels twice as bad as making money feels good (Thaler).
- It doesn't matter what a stock has done in the past. As an investor, you should only be concerned with what a company will deliver in the future.
- A good advisor can add value to their clients by telling them what they need to hear rather than what they want to hear during times of euphoria and depression.
- Home bias is when investors want to put a higher percentage of their portfolio into companies they are familiar with, usually in the countries they live in. This can hinder diversification and unknowingly lead to increased concentration risk.
- It is folly to try and time the market. Far more money has been lost by investors trying to anticipate corrections than has been lost in the corrections themselves. (Lynch)
- You don't have to be the greatest investor to have financial peace of mind, but you do have to avoid the most common behavioral mistakes if you want to achieve your goals. Oftentimes, a coach or financial planner can help you identify and resist these behavioral biases.
- When you think about scratch golfers, it's not necessarily that they make more amazing shots than the rest of us; it's that they make fewer terrible shots than the rest of us. (Murray)

REDEFINING YOUR SECOND HALF

I'm going to tell you a secret, and it's an embarrassing secret. I haven't even shared this with my closest friends. My wife knows, but nobody else really does. Ready? One of my favorite movies in all of cinematography is "The Princess Diaries." You may not be familiar with this film, but I assure you that your granddaughters are. It is the 2001 Disney film about an ordinary teenage girl living in New York City with her single mom who discovers she is not ordinary. Rather, she is the princess and heir to the throne in a small European country called Genovia. One day she believes she is nothing special. She has very ordinary problems, aspirations, and insecurities. The next day, she is royalty. She is the darling of the free world. She now has servants and status and wealth beyond measure. Of course, she was royalty all along; she just didn't know it. Her identity had already been secured. She just had not embraced it yet and was, therefore, living a life that was less than what she was entitled to.[18] Did you know that your story is closer to hers than you may think?

There is a second type of emotional dysfunction that threatens your financial peace of mind. It lies in how you define your worth—your identity. Here we will look at what it means to rediscover your true identity and how doing so frees up your second half of life. To set this up, I want to present the premise that we all have a false identity that we are tempted to buy into, and that is the lie that *you are what you do*.

So much of who we are today seems to be tied to what we do, especially in American culture. I mean, think about that the last time you went to a barbecue. What was the first thing you asked when you met someone new, and what was the first thing they asked you? "So, what do you do?" In any social setting, the first thing we're always tasked with is talking about what we do because that seems to be so critical to who we are. We have had many clients lose that sense of identity when they retire. When they're no longer a part of the law firm they helped build or when they're no longer doing the job they've done for thirty years, they lose who they are, their self-identity, and even their sense of worth. Remember my friend David? He was the attorney who told me, "Eric, after retiring, the only major milestone left for me to do is die."

David's sentiment is part of the reason we regularly research the impact of retirement on mental health, physical health, and mobility. An interesting 2006 study that Kaiser Permanente published in the European Journal of Aging[19] tested a hypothesis that retirement would lead to more prosperity from a mental and physical health standpoint; a higher quality of life. They took two groups of people in the same age bracket, 60 to 66, and the only difference was that one group was retired and the other group was still working. They compared mobility, illness, mental health, and activities of daily living. As I mentioned previously, activities of daily living (ADLs) measure whether you can dress, feed, bathe, use the toilet, and transfer yourself out of bed and into a chair.

When the researchers examined all these empirical metrics, they were trying to prove that retirement leads to greater mental and physical health. What they concluded was that the opposite was true. The retired group within their sample study had lower rates of mobility, higher rates of illness, and worse mental health. Now, I realize there is a difference between correlation and causation, but I firmly believe part of the reason for that decline in quality of life was because so many people buy into the lie, the false identity, that they are what they do. They implicitly believe that when they stop doing, part of them stops being. Part of them dies at retirement because of their false identity.

The reason I want to spend some time discussing your true identity is that I fervently believe your worth and my worth are not at all contingent on what we do or have done. Your worth and my worth are not contingent on what we have accumulated, and we are not the sum of our successes and failures.

We are much more than that. We were made for more, and we'll unpack that more in chapter nine.

> *"Our worth is not at all contingent on what we do or have done. We are not the sum of our successes and failures."*

Why is this important? Why do I devote space here to reject this false identity that our worth is wrapped up in what we do? Well, it's very simple. I have seen the impact when clients choose not to look to their work and accomplishments to define them, and they don't look to their work or accomplishments to provide them with identity. I've seen how when clients reject that false identity, it frees them up to shift their focus from making money to making a difference. They are free to shift from building temporal success for themselves to building a life and legacy of significance through leveraging their time, talent, and treasure into causes that are bigger than themselves.

I've also seen firsthand how this paradigm shift can be life-changing for them. So, this is why I'd rather change the narrative that retirement is the finish line when it should really be the starting point of your second half of life. This moment is your halftime, so I want to ask you, how will you spend the rest of your life? The idea of halftime is a concept popularized by the author, Bob Buford, who coined the phrase, "The halftime of your life is when you move from a life of success to a life of significance."[20]

Let me tell you a little bit about Bob Buford. Bob was a cable TV pioneer in Texas in the late 80s, who made more money than he knew what to do with by the time he was fifty. His only child, whose name was Ross, drowned at the age of twenty-four. That tragedy caused Bob to think about what he wanted his legacy to be. He ended up leveraging all the skills, wisdom, and experience he had gained from his business to help provide strategic consulting to national nonprofits through the Drucker

Institute and the Leadership Network, both of which he led. He said that transition from success to significance was one of the greatest decisions of his lifetime, "Success in the first half is lonely because it is directed inward. It gains significance in the second half from the pouring out of ourselves, our gifts, our talents, our resources."[21]

Not all of us are like Bob Buford, who had the means to chase whatever pursuit was on his mind. Most of us don't have tens of millions of dollars in the bank to launch our "second-half ventures." So what can we do?

Bob raises this question in his book, asking, do you have to be wealthy to pursue halftime? His answer is an unequivocal no. Wherever you are in your career, you can build a parallel outlet of outpouring so that when the time comes for you to transition from the accumulation phase of life to the distribution phase of life, whether that parallel outlet generates income for you or not, it will absolutely generate purpose and significance and satisfaction. So the concept of halftime is not just something for the wealthy. It is something that applies to all of us.

I'll give you an example of a mentor of mine, Tim, who was the CFO of a technology company. One of the things Tim is passionate about is mentoring young fathers when they are in a stage of life where they've been married for about a decade; they've got young kids, and they're starting to get more responsibility at work. That season of life can be packed with increasing pressure and exhaustion. Tim began to have this mentoring passion well before he semi-retired professionally. To him, this activity of mentoring is the thing that brings more joy than any professional success. So when his technology company sold for a large number, his second-half continues to be filled with purpose because his identity was not in his job. Tim still works even though he doesn't need to, but whenever he determines to pivot from the accumulation phase of life to the distribution phase of life, he will continue mentoring young fathers. He will talk them through the stress of having newborn babies and sleep deprivation. He will encourage them to continue communicating well with their wives and pursue and love them during a time in life that tends to bring out the worst in all of us. Mentoring young fathers through that process is a life-giving investment for Tim, and he would say his second half will be a second half of significance because of it.

And again, Tim developed this parallel passion while still working. So when he stops drawing income from an employer and starts drawing his income from his nest egg, mentoring will nourish his soul well beyond his last day at the office.

This is why my colleague Michelle Disney says, "It is just as important to know what you are retiring *to* as it is to know what you are retiring *from*." You may have heard the story of Alfred Nobel, the inventor of dynamite, who was reading the newspaper one day, and to his horror, stumbled upon his own obituary. Now, it turns out his brother had passed away, and the newspaper published Alfred's obituary by mistake. The headline of the obituary read, "The merchant of death is dead,"[22] because Alfred was the inventor of dynamite. It went on to say, "Dr. Alfred Nobel, who became rich by finding ways to kill more people faster than ever before, died yesterday." Now, I want to take a moment. Can you imagine reading that article about yourself and hearing that people were celebrating your death because of your life's work?

> "It is just as important to know what you are retiring to as it is to know what you are retiring from." —Michelle Disney

Well, Dr. Nobel *was* mortified to know how he would be remembered, and at that moment, he determined he would use the bulk of his wealth to establish the Nobel Foundation, which presents international awards and recognition of cultural and scientific achievements. Today, Dr. Alfred Nobel is not remembered as the merchant of death but as the creator of the Nobel Prize and, consequently, as a great humanitarian. Having read his obituary while he was still alive allowed him to change his legacy. So, friends, I want to tell you that right now is your opportunity to change your obituary. Do you need help figuring out what your second half should be? Often, we'll ask that question to clients, and they look at us dumbfounded. Sometimes we'll go through the exercise I've written below, encouraging them to take a moment to think about it right then and there.

Similarly, I want to encourage you to take a moment right here and now. If you could put this book down and take some time to write your ideal obituary, that would be great. Don't worry; I'll wait. I'll be right here when you're done. Write your ideal obituary by answering these questions, or think about these questions in your mind as you write:

1. What do you want to be remembered for? What do you want people to say about you?
2. Who do you hope remembers you and misses you most? What do you want them to say about you?
3. You have developed a treasure trove of knowledge, wisdom, and experiences. How can you leverage those strengths to make a difference in the lives of others in your community? You may not know the people in your community who will be the greatest beneficiaries of your experience and your wisdom, but how can you leverage those?

And then, revisiting the Kinder questions we introduced in the financial plan section of the book, we ask:

1. If money were no object, how would you spend your life?
2. If you had five to ten years to live, how would you spend your time and resources?
3. If you had twenty-four hours to live, what would you wish you had time to do or accomplish? What would you regret that you did not have the opportunity to do?

I want to give you some good news today. As you're reading this, this moment is the starting line of your second half. I'd be willing to bet the primary thing holding you back from your obituary becoming a reality is either fear of one thing or another, or simple inertia. But you can choose, friend, to start right now. As my friend and author Lara Casey says, "You know all those things that you've always wanted to do? You should go do them."[23]

An abundant retirement is not about withdrawing. It is about recreating and re-creating. It's about redeploying all the wisdom and experience you have accumulated into a new context. And that is why we use the phrase "pivot to another passion" rather than just the generic word "retire." So humbly, my contention, and Buford's contention, is that a second half devoted to your leisure pursuits would get really boring after a very short while, whereas a second half devoted to helping yourself by helping others will lead to much higher levels of satisfaction. A study published in 2007 by the University of Michigan in the Journal of Gerontology concluded that people who regularly volunteer their time in retirement increase their life expectancy and heighten their overall zest for living.[24] This is what I've seen in eighteen years of counseling clients as well.

The next time you are at a barbecue, remember that when many people retire, they feel like they lose their identity. They feel like they have lost or will lose what made them who they are, like my lawyer friend David. He is thinking out of his false self, that notion you are what you do. This belief is very prevalent, not just in David but in many other people. Maybe instead of asking them, "What do you do," we can shift our question to "Tell me about your story." Or my favorite, "Nice to meet you, Keith (age 65). What do you want to be when you grow up?" Let them share who they are and what they are passionate about, rather than what they do to put food on the table. How do you spend your free time? What's on your bucket list? What's the greatest adventure you've ever been on? I need some ideas for a family trip. You will get to know them better, and you'll probably find people will prefer to chat with you at parties.

For clients who feel like all they have left to do is die after retirement, we remind them they are so much more than what they do. There's a whole, exciting adventure waiting for them that is theirs to be had if they'll just take some time to think about what that could be and engage in building that parallel passion.

You don't have to wait until the day you pivot to discover that parallel passion, either. It's important to start building that soul-nourishing outlet in the last five to ten years of your career. That way, when you decide to make the transition, you can hit the ground running; you're already well into that secondary passion that's going to be more outward-focused and will provide more significance and satisfaction to your life. Congratulations! You are on your way to making that ideal obituary a reality.

This is probably an appropriate time to say also that you can't change the past. If you've made mistakes in your past or haven't been the greatest father or mother or grandparent, you can't change that, but you can absolutely change what you do from

> *"Whether a parallel outlet generates income for you or not, it will absolutely generate purpose, significance, and satisfaction."*

this moment forward. You've been given today. What you do with that gift is up to you. Tomorrow is not promised to any of us.

If you're reading this and you've already stopped working, maybe you're hearing me say "pivot to another passion," and you haven't pivoted to anything. You've made the transition from accumulation to distribution, but now you're to the point where you wake up every morning, and it's the same day. You're either spending just to spend or letting the hours go by because you have nothing else to do. You would say that the emotional component of your financial peace of mind feels very lethargic and unhealthy. Now is your opportunity to re-engage.

Suppose you're in the first category of what we talked about, of giving in to some of these biases and losing sight of what you can and can't control. In that case, emotional health will come when you trust a data-driven objective process and some of the risk-mitigation techniques we talked about in the previous chapter. I believe that can be one of the greatest takeaways for you. Let me give you an example of this.

Our clients who follow the prescription of having a data-driven plan, use a diversified, balanced portfolio, leverage dividend stocks to generate income, and use a cash flow reserve, so they're not putting themselves in a position to sell when the market is falling, can weather a lot of volatile markets. These are our clients who really buy into the stress-test concept. I'll tell you, in the year 2020, which was the first year of COVID-19, it was amazing for me to see clients call in scared because at one point in time, in March 2020, the S&P fell 35% in one month! Clients felt like their world was falling apart, but we would say to them, "Hey, let's review the financial stress test." "Give me an opportunity to show you that when we stress test your nest egg, this scenario is already baked in, not just the probability, but the certainty that we're going to have periods of time where the market is down 20%, 30%, or 40%."

The COVID-19 pandemic was a shock to me and you, but it was not a surprise to the financial stress test because the test knew we would have turbulent periods like this. It didn't know it would be called COVID-19, but the stress test knew we would have periods where the market would fall 35%. And by anticipating that, we could show clients, after the 35% drop in the market, they're still right on track to be able to spend what they want to spend and give away what they want to give away and leave behind what they want to leave behind.

To see the anxiety lift from their faces has been one of the most rewarding parts of my career. I believe that some of the concepts we talked about, like mitigating risk, are crucial to securing emotional financial peace of mind. Because when you trust a data-driven plan rather than just your gut or a hunch, it's a lot more reliable. And by leaning on that, it's an easy way for us to help clients lift their gaze.

If you are not experiencing emotional peace of mind because of a false identity, I would say to work to embrace the fact that you are not the sum of your accomplishments or the sum of your failures because you're not. You are so much more. You were meant for so much more. The lie of the false identity will steal, kill, and destroy your peace. I don't want that for you. I want you to experience life to the fullest, so keep reading.

We've gone through the *financial* portion of financial peace of mind. We've gone through the *emotional* component of financial peace of mind. Again, this is where 99% of authors and financial planners would conclude our discussion, but we still have two more legs for our financial peace of mind tabletop to cover. And we're going to begin next with relationships because what is more emotional than our relationships with those who are dear to us?

Let's Review

- The notion that you are what you do is a lie and a false identity. You are much more than that.
- Rejecting this false identity is the first step in seeing that retirement is not the finish line but the starting point of your second half of life. Then you are ready to "move from a life of success to a life of significance." (Buford)
- Wherever you are in your career, you can build a parallel outlet of outpouring so that when the time comes for you to transition from the accumulation phase of life to the distribution phase of life. Whether that parallel outlet generates income for you or not, it will absolutely generate purpose, significance, and satisfaction.
- It is just as important to know what you are retiring *to* as it is to know what you are retiring *from*. (Disney)
- Take some time to write your ideal obituary. What do you want to be remembered for? Who do you want to miss you the most? What can you do between now and then to leverage your wisdom and experience to bless others?
- "All those things that you've always wanted to do? You should go do them." (Casey)

Relational Component of FPOM

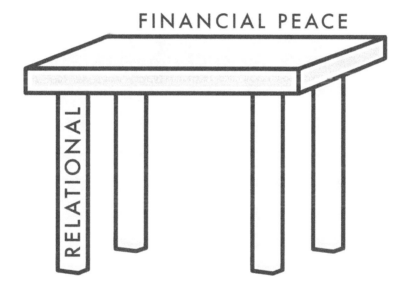

THE RELATIONAL VALUE OF MONEY

I started in wealth management in 2004. Over the years, I've seen how money impacts hundreds of families, and I've drawn some conclusions about money and relational dysfunction. I have observed that money, more often than not, tears families apart rather than brings them together. This does not have to be, nor should it be the case. It is said that intelligence is the ability to learn from your mistakes, whereas wisdom is the ability to learn from the mistakes of others. I am hopeful that you will glean some wisdom in this chapter by examining common missteps people make so you can allow your money to be a blessing to your loved ones rather than a curse.

I am reminded of my friend, Steven, whom I introduced as our archetype of relational dysfunction. Steven used his money to try and wield power over people. He manipulated friends and family members through money, which led to an absence of financial peace of mind relationally. I just want to share with you a couple of statistics that I think are interesting about broken families and estate settlements.

- 55% of Americans die without a will or an estate plan.[25] This really throws a wrench into things. When we don't have any communication around the estate settlement prior to death, it oftentimes leads to arguments and disputes, and sometimes even contested wills.
- 35% of Americans report personally experiencing or knowing someone who has seen family conflict due to not having an estate plan in place.[26]
- The Nevada Law Journal cites that 1% to 3% of all wills are formally contested.[27] Formally contesting a will is a nuclear option where you are making the case that the will is legally invalid. You are suing based on the notion that somehow you're being cheated out of your inheritance.

So how do we sidestep this possibility? How do we go about achieving financial peace of mind relationally? Well, the first step is to put money in its proper place in terms of its purpose and significance. We need to recognize that money is a tool, a means to an end, not an end in and of itself. Money is not an ultimate thing because if it were, more money would always create more happiness. And that's simply not true. Plenty of research suggests there is a diminishing marginal return, that as income and wealth grow, happiness doesn't grow at the same rate.[28] There can be a flattening, a plateauing, or even a decrease, as we'll learn about later on.

Going back to my friend Steven, all of his money could not provide him relational health. What we find is that money is a wonderful servant but a terrible master. It is a helpful tool, but an empty goal.

So how do you know if you are placing too high of a value on money? I think one helpful relational diagnostic is simply to ask yourself the question, "Am I using people as a means to get more money, or am I using money as a means of loving people?" There are a couple of best practices we can talk about with that in mind.

> *How do you know if you are placing too high of a value on money? Ask yourself, "Am I using people as a means to get more money, or am I using money as a means of loving people?"*

Close your eyes for a moment and envision the two of us walking through a beautiful meadow on a hundred-acre plot of farmland paradise. And as we walk and talk, listening to the birds, imagine coming up on a beautiful, immaculate pond next to a quiet wood. It's almost poetic. You can smell the pristine, crystal clear water, the honeysuckle, and the gentle breeze, and you kneel down for a cool, fresh drink of water. It's so peaceful, right?

How would your mental picture change if I told you that the water was stagnant and had nowhere to go, nowhere to flow to? Does this change the picture in your mind? I would guess that now, in your daydream, you're thinking about all the algae and bacteria and the parasites that could be in the water. Suddenly, you're not nearly as thirsty as you thought you were because there's a huge difference between flowing water and stagnant water. Water that flows actively from one place to another is much cleaner, much healthier than water that just sits and stagnates. Interesting fact: the ISME Journal says that it can take as little as six days of stagnation to change the bacterial composition of water completely.[29]

I want to make the argument that wealth is very similar. The wealth that flows through our fingers as a conduit of blessing to others is much healthier than hoarded wealth. Hoarded wealth becomes stagnant and even corrosive. And hoarded wealth has a very real impact on our relational wellbeing. So how can I become a conduit of blessing? How can I allow my wealth to be used as a tool rather than my being held captive by it? That's what this chapter is about: giving. Because I will show you that giving produces relational peace of mind, both for the giver and the recipient, if done well.

Giving to Your Family

There are two major types of giving. One type of giving is *inter vivos*, and the other is testamentary. *Inter vivos* giving means giving done during your lifetime, while testamentary giving is done after your death. You can become a conduit of blessing by giving to your family and community in either of these two ways. In this section, let's look at giving to family, first inter vivos and what that can look like, then we'll dive into testamentary giving.

Eric Chetwood, CFP®

Inter Vivos Giving

If you want to give to your family throughout your lifetime, there are five types of gifts you can make, generally. The added benefit of these types of gifts is that these are tax-free gifts, meaning there is no gift tax that you need to pay and no income the recipient needs to declare.

1. Annual Exclusion

Consider making an annual exclusion gift to your family members. Right now, as I'm writing this in 2022, the annual exclusion is up to $16,000 per person. That is the amount of money you can give to any other individual without having to worry about filing a gift tax return or counting against your combined lifetime gift and estate tax exemption. Couples can double their annual exclusion by giving something called a split gift, which we'll describe below. It requires filing a split gift form, but no tax is owed.

As an example, I can give my son Noah up to $16,000 a year without having to worry about filing a gift tax return. My wife, Allison, can also give him $16,000 a year. So couples together can give up to $32,000 to any individual without that gift counting against their lifetime exclusion, which is the total amount you can pass to heirs without incurring gift tax. This "doubling" is called a split gift.

As I write this in 2022, the lifetime gift and estate tax exclusion amount is $12.06 million per person or $24.12 million per couple. Again, this is the combined amount you could give to heirs over your lifetime and shelter from estate tax at death. I've included a chart below showing the history of that lifetime exclusion. The $12 million current exclusion seems great but as recently as the George W. Bush administration, you could only pass up to $1 million per person. Depending on who is in Congress, the lifetime exclusion can fluctuate dramatically. And that's significant because there are plenty of people in New York or California who are homeowners, and their real estate value alone would put them well above that $1 million exclusion we saw under the Bush administration. This is something to be aware of, even if you don't necessarily consider yourself a high-net-worth individual.

Retire to the Fullest

Historical Estate Tax Exemption Amounts
(per person)

Year	Estate Tax Exemption	Federal Estate Tax Rate
1997	$600,000	55%
1998	$625,000	55%
1999	$650,000	55%
2000	$675,000	55%
2001	$675,000	55%
2002	$1,000,000	50%
2003	$1,000,000	49%
2004	$1,500,000	48%
2005	$1,500,000	47%
2006	$2,000,000	46%
2007	$2,000,000	45%
2008	$2,000,000	45%
2009	$3,500,000	45%
2010	$5,000,000 or $0	35% or 0%
2011	$5,000,000	35%
2012	$5,120,000	35%
2013	$5,250,000	40%
2014	$5,340,000	40%
2015	$5,430,000	40%
2016	$5,450,000	40%
2017	$5,490,000	40%
2018	$11,180,000	40%
2019	$11,400,000	40%
2020	$11,580,000	40%
2021	$11,700,000	40%

source: IRS

It will be interesting to see what happens in the future with the lifetime exclusion. Politically, we need to find ways of paying for our chronic federal budget deficits. I believe that the estate tax will become a more powerful lever, and it will be interesting to see what the lifetime exclusion amount evolves to overtime.

2. Direct Education Funding

A second way to strategically give an *inter vivos* gift is to take advantage of direct education funding. This is where we're funding education in the present. For example, you have a grandchild going to a private school for K-12. Or maybe you have a child or grandchild in college or grad school. If you make a check payable directly to the school, it would be free of gift tax. That amount does not count against your annual exclusion of $16,000.

But if I have a child who is in grad school, and my wife and I write them a check for $32,000, and then they turn around and use that $32,000 to pay for tuition in grad school, that does count against the annual exclusion because it went to them rather than directly to the institution. It would be best to make the check payable directly to the school or university to not count against the annual exclusion. This is important to remember for present education funding.

In terms of future education funding right now, one of the most powerful vehicles you can use is something called a 529 college savings plan. We are often asked if there is a funding ceiling for the 529 plan. The 529 allows you to fund (front-load) up to five years' worth of the annual exclusion before you must worry about gift taxes. With the 529 plan, theoretically, if you're a couple, you could deposit $32,000 per grandchild for five years, which gets you to $160,000 per grandchild that you can invest into the 529. You can allow that money to grow. It'll be invested in mutual funds or a diversified portfolio of companies through mutual funds. As that money grows, it can grow completely income tax-free and also free of capital gains, as long as it's taken out and used for qualified education purposes.

There is a lot of flexibility with these 529 plans if they're set up correctly. The Tax Cuts and Jobs Act of 2018 now allows families to take money out of their 529 plan to fund K–12 private schooling, up to $10,000 per student per year. You can also use 529 plans to fund undergraduate education or graduate school.

One of the most popular questions we get about 529 plans is, "What if my child gets a scholarship?" "What if they decide they don't want to go to college, and we have money left in the 529 at the end of their education?" You can take the amount you contributed out (the principal) and use it for something other than qualified education expenses without incurring tax or penalty, but anytime you start tapping the earnings, you're going to have to pay taxes on those earnings and a 10% penalty.

There are other options available to you as well. If you set up the 529 plan correctly and the educational funding needs of the child change, you can change the beneficiary to one of your other children. Or you could say, "Hey, Johnny, we're proud of you for getting a scholarship. We have set this money aside for your education funding, and because you got a scholarship, we are going to continue to let it grow. Then if you don't need it for grad school, one day when you have kids, we'll change the beneficiary so your kids can be the beneficiary." This is an effective wealth transfer strategy because you're allowing that money to continue to grow completely exempt from taxes, which supercharges the compound growth. So 529s can be a wonderful tool when we're talking about making gifts to your family to fund future education.

3. Paying Medical Bills

The third effective way of making gifts to family members is by paying medical bills on their behalf. And like what we were talking about in the education funding section, you would make the check payable directly to the healthcare provider. Paying the medical facility directly means this transaction is not treated as a gift, and therefore, it does not count against the annual exclusion of what you might give them elsewhere.

4. Investing in Life Experiences

I really love to talk about these next two types of *inter vivos* giving. Investing in life experiences with your family is a great way to give to your family. Many of our client's richest memories are trips and experiences they have shared with their loved ones, so I want to encourage you to take a moment and think through these questions:

- Where have you always wanted to go? Hawaii? The South of France? The Caribbean? National parks out West?
- What have you always wanted to do? Sail the Great Lakes? Horseback ride in the Grand Canyon? Go whale watching in Alaska? Cruise the Danube? Golf in Scotland? Visit boutique wineries in California? Go on safari in the Serengeti?
- With whom would you want to share that experience?

I want you to put together a plan to just go do them. Don't talk about it. Be about it. I've never had a client regret investing in life experiences with loved ones. A good financial plan will help you make it work.

5. Creating and Supporting Opportunities

The final way to make *inter vivos* gifts is something I learned from a client, and I think this is brilliant. I had a client who said, "I remember vividly when I came home one day, and I told my dad that I had seen a bike I really wanted in the store. And my dad said, 'Son, I'm not going to buy you that bike, but I'll give you money so that you can earn money to buy that bike.'"

So the dad went out and bought a lawnmower on behalf of the son, and he allowed the son to mow lawns around the neighborhood so he could earn the money to buy his own bike. And the client said, "I've never forgotten that." I want to submit that idea to you as a wonderful suggestion of making investments in your family, making investments in your kids and grandkids, and showing them the value of hard work and the dignity of being able to earn something on their own. What ways could you invest in individuals in your family to elevate the dignity of work and catalyze entrepreneurship? A slight paradigm shift when it comes to giving could be life-changing for your loved ones.

Testamentary or Legacy Giving

Now let's move to the types of gifts you can give after your death, called testamentary or legacy giving. It's a good thing to give money to your kids and grandkids. Proverbs 13:22 says that a good man leaves an inheritance to his children's children. Yet, I have seen in practice that we want to hold that in tension with the notion that too much inheritance to children or grandchildren can become more of a curse than a blessing.

My business partner, Rick Adams, once told me, "I want to leave my kids enough money that they can do whatever they want to do. If they want to devote their lives to digging wells in Africa, I want to support them in that. But I don't want to leave them so much money that they don't have to do anything productive with their lives." And I think that's a good tension to hold—an inheritance is a good thing, but there comes the point where an inheritance becomes more of a curse than a blessing. That threshold will differ for each family, so we encourage our clients to think, pray through, and talk about it with their spouses.

So how do we do this well? There are four keys to effective legacy giving. If you follow these principles, your legacy giving will be smooth, clear, and manageable, allowing you to address any tension before it could spiral out of control. You're apt to create a recipe for confusion, poor communication, and relational contention without these keys.

> *"An inheritance is a good thing, but there comes the point where an inheritance becomes more of a curse than a blessing."*

Let me give you an illustration to make my point. Imagine a football coach rallying his team on the side of the field saying, "All right, guys. Go run the play." And his team looks at him, confused, and says, "Well, Coach, which play?" The coach responds, "Come on, guys, you know. Go score a touchdown." And they say, "Well, do you want us to run the ball or pass the ball?" The coach, growing frustrated, says, "Guys, you are professional football players. Just run the play." You can see how this would not lead to a successful outcome.

We saw earlier in the chapter that contestability is more common than you might think. I've seen beneficiaries get so overwhelmed trying to settle an estate because the now-deceased patriarch or matriarch wanted to avoid discussing or making an estate plan. Understandably, it is awkward to talk to family about their eventual death, and it is hard to think about their own mortality. So they put it off. Their heirs are left with, "Go run the play." However, clear communication mitigates confusion and frustration.

Let's explore these four principles for legacy giving so that you can have an effective game plan.

1. Organization

On the organizational side, I think it's important to put together a folder that has five basic elements of organization:

- *Net worth statement.* We discussed this in chapter 2. List out everything you own, including your checking account, savings account, house, car, 401(k), IRAs, all your real estate. Then list out everything you owe, like the mortgage on your house and investment properties, credit card debt, and other loans. Take the value of everything you own, subtract out the amount of everything you owe, and that's going to give your net worth. This statement is helpful to your heirs, your executor, and your CPA, as it allows them to see what you're worth at a glance on one page. Ideally, that net worth statement is going to list out where those accounts are held. For example, I have this account at Schwab or Fidelity, this piece of real estate at this address, and so forth. For a sample net worth statement, see appendix 3.
- *Contact page.* Let your heirs know the names and contact information for your financial advisor, CPA, estate attorney, and life insurance agent, so they know who to call when the time comes. These will be very important and will make it easy on your heirs or your executor as they're going through your estate administration.
- *List of life insurance policies.* This list needs to include the following data: which company the policy is with (Prudential, John Hancock, Transamerica, etc.). Write out the policy numbers, the face amounts, and how long you expect those policies to be in force. Is the policy for a death benefit of $100K? $1 million? $2 million? Do you expect the policy to be in effect until 2030? 2040?
- *Estate documents.* These are the documents your attorney puts together, such as your last will and testament, your power of attorney document, your healthcare power of attorney document,

any trust documents, and a living will, which we'll talk about more soon. If you don't have these documents, engage an attorney to prepare them for you before this Thanksgiving. Your heirs will be *thankful* you did. See what I did there?

- *Most recent tax return.* This will be very helpful to your executor, your financial planner, and your CPA as they go through your estate administration.

2. Open Communication

The second key to effective testamentary giving is to have a policy of open communication. And I know when I write this, it will be somewhat controversial because people don't want their kids to know what they own. They don't want their kids looking forward to their death. But let me tell you a story of one of my clients.

My client wasn't an estate attorney, but he got his kids together and said, "Hey, guys, I want to tell you how we are going to divide this estate. I want to tell you in advance who will get what and who will serve as our executor. And I want you to hear it from me because I want you to hear my rationale for dividing things the way I did. I want you to hear loud and clear that I won't tolerate any fighting or squabbling over this. Our family bond is much more valuable than any amount of money or material possessions. I would just as soon light all these possessions on fire before I would allow it to tear my family apart."

Knowing that clear communication mitigates confusion and frustration, my client was willing to initiate an awkward conversation that was a little bit unpleasant to spare his family from years of fighting, which would have been very unpleasant.

You can add a legal term to your will or trust that I would encourage you to talk about with your attorney. It's called the "contestability clause." Basically, it says, in writing, "Hey, kids, if you object to the legal validity of the will because you think somehow you're being cheated out of what is rightfully yours, then let me say here, in the will, that you will get nothing if you formally contest the will." It can be a very effective tool to force siblings to get along.

3. Legal Efficacy

You want to ensure you have legal efficacy, which means that the legal documents you have in place are congruent with your wishes. It does you no good to come up with estate planning strategies that are legally impotent. These five documents are a great place to begin with your Certified Financial Planner® or estate attorney:

- *Explicit and updated beneficiaries.* Make sure you have explicit and updated primary and contingent beneficiaries on all your life insurance policies, IRAs, 401(k)s, etc. This is the clearest and easiest way to ensure your assets are going where you want them to go.
- *Will.* A will is a legal document that expresses a person's wishes as to how their property will be distributed after their death and which person will manage the property until its final distribution. The will is wonderful, but it's set up to be a catchall, governing everything that doesn't have an explicit beneficiary.
- *Power of Attorney.* For an effective legal strategy, make sure you have a power of attorney document, which is simply a written authorization that someone else will represent you or act on your behalf if you become incapacitated. Today, many hospitals require a separate power of attorney for healthcare decisions, so make sure to prepare a separate healthcare power of attorney document.
- *Living Will.* This is another document of instructions that you provide in advance to the person making healthcare decisions on your behalf due to illness or incapacity.
- *Revocable Trust.* The revocable trust is a private substitute for a public will. It can also serve as a catchall. A will is a public document, meaning when you die, the probate court reads your will and talks about how you want your assets distributed publicly, whereas a revocable trust is a private process. And because it's revocable, you can change it at any point in time.

4. Minimize Estate Taxes if You are High Net Worth (Optional)

The final key to effective testamentary giving is to minimize taxes, starting with estate taxes. This discussion is primarily going to apply to you if you find yourself above the lifetime exclusion. As we've said, the 2022 amount is $12.06 million per person. The Biden administration has said they'd like that amount to be closer to $3.5 million per person. If your net worth is above $3.5 million per person or $7 million per couple, this section may apply to you. Otherwise, you can skip this section and go to the next one on giving to your community.

In the event that you find you are above the lifetime exclusion, you'll want to discuss a couple of different trust mechanisms with your estate attorney to get assets out of your estate. It's important to understand that only assets in an Irrevocable Trust (a trust you cannot change and sometimes even control) are removed from your taxable estate. In contrast, assets in a Revocable Trust (a trust you can change and control) are not removed from your taxable estate. Your goal is to get your taxable estate below the lifetime gift and estate tax exclusion amount. This is important because every dollar above the lifetime exclusion amount will be subject to federal estate taxes at a rate of 40% (as of 2022)! In addition, some states have their own inheritance tax, which would be assessed along with the 40%. So, as you can see, prudent estate planning can mean huge tax savings for your family.

With a little creative thinking, you can reduce or avoid estate taxes. Close your eyes with me and think of a gallon pitcher. Imagine you have five gallons of water you want to store, but a gallon pitcher is the only tool you have to transport them. For the sake of our illustration, each family is limited to owning only one of these pitchers. If you try to pour all five gallons of water into your pitcher at once, anything above that gallon is going to be wasted. But, if you fill that gallon pitcher and redeploy it five different times, then you can spread out your five gallons and minimize the waste. How would you do that? Maybe you go out and buy four decorative water fountains. You can fill and redeploy your gallon pitcher four separate times and still be able to enjoy five gallons of water, having only used your gallon pitcher to distribute the water. Whatever the lifetime exclusion number is the amount that you can fill your "pitcher" and pass directly to your kids at the end of your life. Anything above that can be redeployed into certain types of trusts that are represented by our water fountains. Our heirs and charities can still enjoy monetary benefits from our trusts while abiding by the constraints of only using one "pitcher."

Three different trusts may be worth talking about with your estate attorney as you're trying to get under that lifetime exclusion amount. These three trusts are examples of an Irrevocable Trust. As a refresher, there are two components of an irrevocable trust. The first component is the income generated and distributed to some income beneficiary. The other component is the remainder amount that is left to the remainder beneficiary. Each component is answering the questions, "Who receives the income over a set of years," and, "Who receives the remaining principal at the end of those years, and how?" The income beneficiary and the remainder beneficiary do not have to be the same person, and usually, they are not the same person.

- *Grantor-Retained Annuity Trust (GRAT).* This is one of the greatest tools we might use to get under the lifetime exclusion. Let's say my current net worth is $9 million, and Congress has set the lifetime exclusion at $7 million per couple, so I need to get $2 million out of my estate and into a creative "fountain," so to speak. It would be nice to draw income and dividends off of that $2 million, so I set up a GRAT, fund it with $2 million, and irrevocably determine that my spouse can receive a fixed amount of income for ten years. Whatever is leftover at the end of those ten years goes to our kids. By setting up a GRAT and moving $2 million into it, I now own $7 million worth of stuff and a separate irrevocable trust that I no longer have control over owns $2 million worth of stuff. By moving this $2 million out of my control, I save approximately 40% of federal estate taxes, which is $800,000. This is a simple way that a GRAT can get money out of your estate and still generate income that will go to the people you want it to go to. You can still receive income from that trust, and your heirs can be the remainder beneficiaries. However, it's important to note that if you die within the income period (ten years, in our example), the assets in the GRAT will be included in your taxable estate. Thus, you'll want to work closely with an estate attorney and Certified Financial Planner® to select an appropriate timeframe where the income funds your needs, but you are not in reasonable danger of dying before the end of the term.

- *Charitable Remainder Trust (CRT)*. This is a similar concept to the one above, in that if my total assets are above the lifetime exclusion by $2 million, I could theoretically put $2 million into a charitable remainder trust. I might be eligible to receive a tax deduction for up to some percentage of my adjusted gross income. I can receive that tax deduction immediately, and I can still draw income off that trust and receive dividends and interest. But at the end of my life, in exchange for that upfront tax deduction, the remainder of the trust would have to go to a qualified charity or combination of charities of my choosing. I've thus removed $2 million from my taxable estate, still received income off of that $2 million, and fulfilled a charitable giving goal at death.

- *Qualified Personal Residence Trust (QPRT)*. This might be where you would put your home or maybe your beach house into a trust. Similar to being an income beneficiary, you can still use that beach house for a set number of years, but it would pass to your remainder beneficiaries at the end of the trust term. Designating those beneficiaries is an irrevocable decision. This is particularly strategic if you live in an area of the country where property values are very high. For example, if you live in Brooklyn or San Francisco and own a home. It may be that while your home is not necessarily extravagant, the value pushes you well over the lifetime exclusion if you were to leave the real estate directly to your kids. By putting it in a trust first, you get that inflated value out of your estate, and you are able to leave more of your liquid assets directly to your kids.

So all three of these types of trusts are things you can talk about with your estate attorney. I need to say that I am not an attorney, and I am not giving legal advice in this book. I am simply trying to put together ideas that you can run by your estate attorney to see if they make sense for you.

Eric Chetwood, CFP®

Giving to Your Community

Now let's also discuss the importance of making lifetime gifts to your community and why this is important. In the book *How to Be Rich* by Andy Stanley, a Gallup study polled people from many different socioeconomic classes. The study asked them if they thought they were rich, and a strange phenomenon occurred. Very few Americans felt as though they were rich,

> *"Statistically, the financial disparity between you and Bill Gates is smaller than the disparity between you and the rest of the world."*[31]

and when they were asked, "Well, what would it take for you to feel rich?" the majority of them said that if their income doubled, then they would feel rich.[30]

So, for example, the family making $50,000 felt like, "Ooh, if we can only make $100,000, then we would be rich." And the family making $100,000 thought if they were making $200,000, then they would be rich, and so on and so forth. In light of that, I want to share with you a mind-blowing statistic. If you make more than $41,000 in a given year, you are in the top 1% of global income. Let me say that in a different way. Statistically, the financial disparity between you and Bill Gates is smaller than the disparity between you and the rest of the world.[31] This fact is amazing to me.

The same study asked people if they felt like they were generous, and a large majority answered, "Yes, of course, I'm generous." Yet, when examining their giving, the average giving was less than 4% of their adjusted gross income. So this study concludes that many Americans feel like they are not rich, and yet, indisputably, they are. And many Americans feel like they are generous, and yet, statistically, they are not.[32]

Why is this? While we may say it is better to give than receive, especially during Thanksgiving and Christmas, Americans functionally live their lives as if the opposite is true. We live as though it is better to receive than give, which begs our discussion question: Is it actually good for you to give wealth away? Now, what if I were able to show you academic research that found generosity to be just as healthy for you and gave you as big of a rush of energy as going out for a daily jog?[33] Is it really possible that it is to your benefit to willingly part with the wealth you have worked so hard to accumulate?

The answer, friend, is yes. It is empirically, objectively, and academically in your best interest to give away your time, talent, and treasure to causes that cannot repay you or benefit you in any way. Let's examine the work of the Science of Generosity Project based out of the University of Notre Dame, in particular, "The Paradox of Generosity," by Christian Smith and Hilary Davidson. What did they find in their research? Well, I'll quote you a summary from the excellent book, *God and Money*.

> "First of all, giving is good for you. Really good for you. Intentional and regular practices of generosity have been associated with a release of a slew of good chemicals, including oxytocin, dopamine, and various endorphins. These chemicals are the same ones released after a hard workout or after a particularly pleasurable experience. In fact, generosity is strongly and clearly associated with a sense of purpose in life, personal happiness, and overall personal health. Giving, it turns out, lifts up human health as much as aspirin protects the heart.
>
> "Finally, giving even activates the same portion of the brain that lights up when winning the lottery or getting a raise. You may not be able to control when you get a raise, but you can feel just as good simply by engaging in regular, consistent generosity…Conversely, a lack of giving is bad for you. Those who do not regularly give have been found to harbor higher levels of distress hormone, cortisol, which has a linkage to everything from headaches, to stroke, to depression. What other areas suffer when we live non generously? How about pain management, body temperature regulation, blood pressure, and the control of fear. The reality is that living self-indulgent and self-absorbed lives is literally killing us in the affluent West."[34]

The conclusion I'd like to make here, friend, is that it is better to give than receive. Making generous gifts to both family and community that require personal sacrifice empirically leads to higher levels of happiness and greater financial peace of mind. Now let's talk about how to apply that.

I'm going to give you five ways to give to your community. I'll rank them in order from a tax-planning perspective, from the most effective to the least effective.

1. Redirecting Required Minimum Distributions

A required minimum distribution is simply the amount of money that the IRS requires you to withdraw from a traditional IRA, SEP IRA, SIMPLE IRA, or 401K at a certain retirement age. Historically, the age you needed to begin taking your required minimum distribution was seventy and a half. That age has gone up over the last few years. So if you have not already begun taking your required minimum distribution, you may be able to wait until you are seventy-two.

If you're not using that required minimum distribution for living expenses, one of the most effective ways to give generously to your community is simply to ask your financial advisor to redirect those funds so they don't come to you but go directly to your charity of choice. This is something called a *qualified charitable distribution*, defined as a direct transfer of funds from your IRA custodian, payable to a qualified charity. In addition to the benefits of giving to the charity, a qualified charitable distribution excludes the amount donated from your taxable income, unlike regular withdrawals from an IRA.

Usually, every dollar you take out of an IRA and put in your checking account will be a taxable dollar to you and taxed as ordinary income. By sending that money directly to the charity, you are not taking hold of it, and therefore, you are not responsible for paying taxes on it. So a qualified charitable distribution is a great way to give money to charity.

2. Appreciated Stocks

The second most effective means to give to your community is to give appreciated stock to your church or charity of choice. If you buy shares of a company, and you buy them for $50 a share, and they appreciate to $80 a share, you have a $30 profit. If you sell those shares, you will have to pay capital gains tax on that profit. Instead of giving cash or a check to your charity of choice, gift those shares of appreciated stock.

Retire to the Fullest

This accomplishes two things. Number one, if you itemize your taxes, you get the itemized deduction, which is just the amount of the gift times your tax rate. And then the second benefit is that you get to sidestep the tax on the $30 worth of profit or the capital gain. So gifting appreciated stock is almost a double tax benefit as opposed to simply writing a check or giving cash.

3. Donor-advised Fund

If you're unsure which charity you want to give to this year, you can give that appreciated stock (or ownership interest in a building or business) to a donor-advised fund. A donor-advised fund is like a charitable investment account for the sole purpose of supporting charitable organizations you care about.

So when you contribute appreciated stock, other assets, or even cash to a donor-advised fund, you are generally eligible to take an immediate tax deduction, even if you distribute those funds to the ultimate recipient of a church or charity at a later year. You can take the tax deduction this year, then those funds can be invested within the donor-advised fund for tax-free growth. And then, you can recommend grants to virtually any qualified public charity immediately or at a later point in time.

4. Charitable Remainder Trust

We've already talked about this strategy a little bit: the charitable remainder trust or CRT. Again, this is a vehicle that entails a donor placing a major gift of cash or property into a trust. The trust then pays a fixed amount of income each year to the donor. Then when the donor dies, the remainder of the trust is transferred to charity. One of the immediate benefits of this strategy is that when you transfer assets into the trust, you receive a partial income tax deduction for the estimated present value of the remainder interest that will go to charity.

An example of where this might be prudent is if you have concentrated employee stock. You've been working at a company all your life and accumulated a lot of company stock. You can donate that stock into a charitable remainder trust, and you're eligible for a tax benefit upfront. You can sell that appreciated stock within the CRT and diversify into income-producing companies without paying capital gains, drawing income for the rest of your life. Then the balance would go to charity at your death.

The main difference between the donor-advised fund and the charitable remainder trust is that you can receive income from the charitable remainder trust. Whereas with a donor-advised fund, it's easier to set up and cheaper to administer, but you're not able to receive income.

5. Giving Cash

Cash is the easiest way to give but the least effective from a tax-planning perspective. Writing a check or giving cash allows you to be eligible for an itemized deduction if you itemize, but this is not always a given. You also miss out on two things. You do not get to sidestep any capital gains in your stock portfolio. You also lose the flexibility of being able to receive a deduction this year even though the charity might not receive the funds until future years like you would with a charitable remainder trust or donor-advised fund.

Friend, we have established that giving to others is really good for you. We've seen that giving to family and charity through strategic and tax-efficient mechanisms is worth the bit of extra planning. My hope in sharing these best practices around giving to your family and community is that you will be able to utilize these tools to be a conduit of blessing and, thereby, experience financial peace of mind *relationally*.

That brings us to our final section on how money impacts us—*spiritually*. Once again, I estimate that 90% of books about retirement would have ended with the first section on financial best practices. Of the remaining 10%, most of those would have concluded after the discussion on emotional health. The very few that would have mentioned relational health as a necessary component for financial peace of mind would stop there. We are entering uncharted waters as we touch on the spiritual component of money, which is probably the one I'm most excited about. Let's complete the journey toward comprehensive financial peace of mind.

Let's Review

- Money is a tool, a means to an end, not an end in and of itself. Do not let it rule your heart. Money is a wonderful servant but a terrible master.
- Am I using people as a means to get more money, or am I using money as a means of loving people?
- The wealth that flows through our fingers as a conduit of blessing to others is much healthier than wealth that is hoarded. Hoarded wealth becomes stagnant and even corrosive.
- Giving produces relational peace of mind, both for the giver and the recipient if done well.
- Investing in life experiences with your family is a great way to give to your family. Many of our client's richest memories are trips and experiences they have shared with their loved ones.
- An inheritance is a good thing, but there comes the point where too much inheritance becomes more of a curse than a blessing.
- Clear communication about your final wishes mitigates confusion and frustration.
- If you make more than $41,000 in a given year, you are in the top 1% of global income. (Stanley)
- "The financial disparity between you and Bill Gates is smaller than the disparity between you and the rest of the world." (Stanley)

Spiritual Component of FPOM

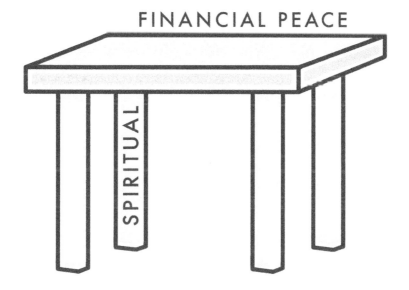

WE ALL WORSHIP SOMETHING

"What good will it be for someone to gain the whole world, yet forfeit their soul?"[35]
(Matthew 16:26)

This brings us to the final section on achieving financial peace of mind, how money impacts us spiritually. Many of you reading this may believe there is no place for a spiritual discussion when we talk about financial planning, and that's okay. I humbly ask that you simply consider this chapter as food for thought. Why do I include this section? You probably bought this book to learn how to accumulate more money because you thought more money would make you happier, but I've seen time and again that money does not satisfy. Some of the wealthiest people I know are some of the most unhappy people I know. It's as if they're drinking the saltwater of success, and it leaves them more and more thirsty. There are also plenty of historical examples of people who have had lots of money and would agree with me that money doesn't satisfy the deepest longings of our hearts. Let me give you one example from history—King Solomon.

A little bit of research will show you that Solomon had an inflation-adjusted net worth of $2 trillion. As I'm writing this, nobody in the world comes close to that. To put it in perspective, if you combined the net worth of Jeff Bezos, Bill Gates, and Warren Buffett, and you multiplied that collective net worth by five, you'd still be $150 billion short of the net worth of King Solomon. He had it all. And yet he famously chronicled in Ecclesiastes 2:10–11, "I denied myself nothing my eyes desired; I refused my heart no pleasure. My heart took delight in all my labor, and this was the reward for all my toil. Yet when I surveyed all that my hands had done and what I had toiled to achieve" (a.k.a. the $2 trillion net worth he had), "everything was meaningless, a chasing after the wind."[36]

Money does not satisfy.

I'll further argue that success does not satisfy. During an interview from Tom Brady with 60 Minutes correspondent Steve Kroft in June of 2005, Steve was talking to Tom about his success on and off the field after he had won his third Super Bowl. What he said about being satisfied in life surprised everyone. Tom Brady said, and I quote, "Why do I have three Super Bowl rings and still think there's something greater out there for me? I mean, maybe a lot of people would say, 'Hey man, this is what it is. I reached my goal. I reached my dream, my life.' Me, I think, 'it's got to be more than this.' I mean, this can't be what it's all cracked up to be. I mean, I've done it. And what else is there for me?" Steve Kroft asked, "Well, Tom, what's the answer to that?" And Brady said, "I wish I knew. I wish I knew."[37]

Think of the thousands of business executives who have intimated something along the lines of, "I spent my entire life climbing the ladder of success, sacrificing friends and family along the way, only to get to the top and realize that my ladder was leaning against the wrong building."

Success does not satisfy.

What about fame? Surely being famous satisfies, doesn't it? There are many quotes we could talk about here, but I'll only share a few with you. Lady Gaga said, "I don't think I could think of a single thing that's more isolating than being famous."[38] Van Morrison of The Doors said, "Being famous was extremely disappointing for me. When I became famous, it was a complete drag, and it is still a complete drag."[39]

Jesse Eisenberg said, "The only way to be turned off to being famous is to be famous."[40] And then finally, Jim Carrey, who we all know and love, said, "I think everybody should get rich and famous and do everything that they ever dreamed of so that they can see that it's not the answer."[41]

Fame does not satisfy.

So, friends, money doesn't satisfy. Success doesn't satisfy. Fame doesn't satisfy. Pleasure does not satisfy either. And it reminds me of a quote from C.S. Lewis who said, and I'll paraphrase, that if we find ourselves with a desire that nothing in this world can satisfy, the most probable explanation is that we were made for more than this world can offer. Maybe we were created for another world.[42]

I know saying this sounds odd to some of you, but again, I humbly ask you to consider the following. I'd like to make the argument that *all of us* functionally live our lives in devotion to something. And it may be that we live our lives in devotion to ourselves. We may live our lives in devotion to God or money or pleasure or comfort or success or family, but all of us "worship" something with our time, talent, and treasure, hoping it will satisfy and fulfill our deepest longings.

I'll use myself as an example. When I was twenty years old, I was living for myself: comfort, pleasure, success, and religion. I wanted it all and devoted my life to get it all. For all intents and purposes, I was a hypocritical Pharisee for the first twenty years of my life.

Then my life was shattered when I was diagnosed with a fairly aggressive form of cancer, and I faced the reality that tomorrow wasn't promised to me. I wondered what would happen if I were to die at age twenty. Would I just disappear? Would I be reincarnated? Would I go to heaven? Would they even let me into heaven? Had I done more good things in my life than bad things? And though I recited Sunday school platitudes to answer some of these questions, these were all questions that haunted me on a soul level because I was staring down the barrel of my own mortality. I was terrified.

So I started searching for answers and found authors like Josh McDowell and Lee Strobel, who had been on similar searches. They had investigated the historical life of Jesus and the empirical evidence for His claims to be the Jewish Messiah.

When you think of the person of Jesus, many of you reading this might envision, as I did, a meek and mild man who was a really nice guy and a pretty good teacher, but then I ran across this quote from C.S. Lewis, and it rattled me. Lewis says,

> I am trying here to prevent anyone saying the really foolish thing that people often say about Jesus. They say, 'I'm ready to accept Jesus as a great moral teacher, but I don't accept His claim to be God.' This is the one thing that we must not say because a man who was merely a man and said the sort of things that Jesus said would not be a great moral teacher. He would either be a lunatic on the level with the man who says he is a poached egg, or else he would be a liar on the level of the devil of hell. You must make your choice. Either this man was, and is, the son of God, or else a madman or something worse. You can shut him up for a fool. You can spit at him and kill him as a demon, or you can fall at His feet and call him Lord and God, but let us not come with any patronizing nonsense about His being a great human teacher. He has not left that open to us. He did not intend to.[43]

Friends, that quote shattered my paradigm of Jesus. I learned that Jesus at least claimed to satisfy my heart in a way that money and success and pleasure never could. He even said, "I have come, Eric, that you may have life and life to the fullest" (John 10:10, paraphrase mine). The Greek word He used there for "fullest" describes a comprehensive and internal satisfaction, which I had been looking for the whole time.

So here's why this is important. Let me zoom out for a moment and provide a slightly larger context because Jesus' offer to make each of us fully alive may be the greatest news ever heard. We'll see. You've probably heard the term "gospel" (i.e., the Gospel of Jesus, the Gospel of John). The word gospel simply means "the good news." So here is the unfiltered good news of Jesus: God created each of us to know Him and enjoy Him forever. But all of us, including you and I, rejected the one who created us, and instead, we lived our lives for ourselves. We have broken most, if not all, of the ten commandments in our hearts and have fallen short of God's standard of perfect holiness. And in doing so, you and I have committed cosmic treason.

The biblical word for our treason is sin, and the penalty for that sin is eternal separation from God and all the wonderful things that are a fruit

Retire to the Fullest

of His presence. That is really bad news for us. Even worse, we cannot cleanse ourselves of this sin any more than a newborn can change his own diapers, but God did not want it to end there.

Here's the good news. God did for us what we could never do for ourselves. He sent His Son, Jesus, to live the perfect, sinless life that we were powerless to live and then to die the death that you and I deserved to die because of our sin. God did not send Jesus to condemn us but to save us through Him. Jesus physically and historically died on a cross in your place and mine so that our penalty would be paid once and for all.

He gave His life as our ransom and then rose from the grave to prove that He had defeated sin's power over us when He bought our freedom. That is the Gospel of Christ in so many words. To say it in a more succinct way, the gospel in four words is "Jesus in my place." And friend, this is amazing news for you and me, and it has huge implications—financial, relational, emotional, and spiritual. Let me be quick to say that I'm not talking about religion here. This is something fundamentally different. As pastor J.D. Greear said,

> "This principle of substitution, Jesus in my place, separates Jesus' gospel from every other religion. The great religions of the world all teach that you must do something to please God. Go here, say this, rub this, touch that, do this, don't do that, pray this, chant that. And if you do these things often enough or well enough, God will accept you, or so you hope. The Gospel, on the other hand, is about what Jesus has done for you. In every other religion, the prophet is a teacher who gives you a plan to earn God's favor. In Christianity, you get the story of a savior who has earned God's favor for you and gives it to you as a gift. You can spell religion D-O. You can spell the Gospel D-O-N-E. Religion requires you to 'do' something to be accepted, whereas the gospel declares you accepted once

"Religion requires you to 'do' something to be accepted, whereas the gospel declares you accepted once you receive what Jesus has 'done' on your behalf."—J.D. Greear

you receive what Jesus has 'done' on your behalf. It's that simple."[44]

So why did I include the Gospel of Jesus in a book about financial planning? Because financial planning looks very different if you have a time horizon of eighty years versus a time horizon of eighty million years. Jesus said in Matthew 6:19–21, "Do not store up for yourselves treasures on earth, where moth and rust destroy, and where thieves break in and steal. But store up for yourselves treasures in heaven, where neither moth nor rust destroys, and where thieves do not break in or steal; for where your treasure is, there your heart will be also."[45]

Our hearts have a way of following our treasure, and that should be somewhat intuitive. If you buy a lake house tomorrow, you're going to start thinking about boats and jet skis and life jackets and furniture and when you can go there next. In fact, every time you have a day off of work or a long weekend, you'll feel somewhat obligated to go to the lake house because your heart has a way of following your treasure. That following or attraction or you might even say that seduction is why wealth and money are like fire. It has great potential for both good and harm. As humans, you and I are particularly susceptible to the temptation to fall in love with money. Our character is incredibly vulnerable to its corrosive influence. That's why Proverbs 30:8 rings so true with me—Lord, give me neither poverty nor riches. That's another reason why giving is good for us, both on a relational level and spiritual level.

The authors of *God and Money* say that giving generously breaks the power of money over our hearts, "The love of money causes us to become insecure, unsatisfied, and self-absorbed. It deceives us into embracing a false system for measuring our self-worth, and conversely, being generous with our wealth eliminates money's power over us."[46]

They conclude that our question should not be how much money should I give, but rather we should humbly ask how much money should I keep. And friends, that's a bold question to ask. It only makes sense to give generously in light of an eternal perspective.

Consider this example from Randy Alcorn's *Treasure Principle*. He says, "Imagine you're alive at the end of the Civil War, and you're living in the South, but you're a Northerner. You plan to move home as soon as the war is over. And while in the South, you've accumulated lots of Confederate dollars, lots of Confederate currency. Now, suppose you know, for a fact, that the North is going to win the war and the end is imminent. What will you do with all of your Confederate currency? If you're smart, there's only one answer. You should immediately cash in your Confederate dollars for US dollars because that is the only money that will have any value once the war is over. And then you would keep only enough Confederate currency to meet your short-term needs. Hoarding dollars and euros and yen makes little sense if you subscribe to an eternal perspective." This is why Alcorn concludes in *The Treasure Principle* the idea that you can't take it with you. You can't take your earthly wealth with you, but you can send it on ahead by storing up treasures in heaven.[47]

But there is one final reason why the spiritual facet of money will compel us to be generous—because Jesus was generous with us. I want to explore a verse in 2 Corinthians 8:9, which says, "For you know the grace of our Lord Jesus Christ, that though he was rich, yet for your sake he became poor, so that you through his poverty might become rich."[48]

Unpack that with me, if you will. Jesus, though He was rich, became poor for our sake so that we, through His poverty, might become rich. That sounds beautifully poetic, but how in the world do we become rich through His poverty? This idea is something theologians call "The Great Exchange." Let me give you a story to illustrate this concept.

On the day I married my wife, Allison, all that was mine became hers, and all that was hers became mine. My little bit of wealth became hers. Also, all my debts became her debts. All of my strengths and weaknesses, my successes and failures, came with me into our marriage and vice versa with her to me. We were united or made one together in marriage. And it was not an even exchange, as I'm well aware of the fact that I married up; I out-punted my coverage, so to speak.

> *"We have this great exchange where Jesus takes all of our sin and shame and insecurity and replaces those things with His perfection and purity and humble confidence. All that is mine becomes His, and all that is His becomes mine."*

But similarly, when we surrender our lives to Christ and are spiritually united with Him, everything that is mine becomes His, and everything that is His becomes mine. What did I bring to the table? Well, I brought my sin, my shame, my selfishness, my insecurity. What did Jesus bring to the table? He brought righteousness, purity, perfection.

We have this great exchange where Jesus takes all of our sin and shame and insecurity and replaces those things with His perfection and purity and humble confidence. All that is mine becomes His, and all that is His becomes mine. This is why Romans 8:1 says there is no condemnation for those who are in Christ because, in Christ, our spiritual poverty is replaced with His spiritual perfection.[49] As Tim Keller says, "The gospel says that you are more sinful and flawed than you ever dared believe, but more accepted and loved than you ever dared hope."[50] That is what makes amazing grace so amazing.

So let me land the plane here, friends. We all worship something. You and I were created to live in fellowship with the God of the universe. We were created to worship Him. And though our own rebellion hopelessly separates us from Him, Jesus has reconciled us to God with His own blood. The ransom has already been paid. The only decision we have to make is whether or not we will accept that ransom as a free gift or whether we want to pay it on our own. Keep in mind that a gift is only an offer until it is received. Will you receive it? It costs you nothing, yet it requires total surrender, like a rebel laying down his arms.

You may be asking how to go about surrendering. You can pray something like this, and keep in mind there's nothing magical about these words. You're just talking to God like you would a close friend, and you might say something like, "Dear Lord Jesus, I know that I'm a sinner, and I ask for your forgiveness. I believe you died for my sins and rose from the dead. I turn from my sins and invite you to come into my heart and life. I want to trust and follow you as my Lord and Savior."

As we close out our discussions, I want to give you some questions to ponder as you reflect on what we've talked about regarding the spiritual aspects of money. Do you believe that Jesus has done everything necessary to save you from your sin? Are you willing to do whatever He tells you to do and go wherever He tells you to go? If your answer is yes, I am delighted to tell you that the Bible declares you free, clean, reconciled, and there is no condemnation for those in Christ. You are now a new creation. Though your sins and rebellion were as scarlet, you have been made as pure as snow.

The old you is gone along with your shame and your guilt. You are now totally known *and* totally loved.

You have been reconciled to the God of the universe who doesn't want religion from you. He wants a personal relationship with you, and you can get to know Him by reading His love letter to you in the Bible and praying to Him or talking with Him, just like you would any other friend. You might start in the book of Mark to read about Jesus' life, death, and resurrection in your place.

If you surrendered your life to Jesus for the first time, I would love to send you some additional resources. I've included my contact information at the website www.retiretothefullest.com. I would love to encourage you as you begin this exciting journey.

That is why I included the Gospel of Jesus in a book about money—I have seen so many people look to money to fill a void that can only be satisfied in Jesus. As Dietrich Bonhoeffer says, "Christianity preaches the infinite worth of that which is seemingly worthless and the infinite worthlessness of that which is seemingly so valued."[51]

Friends, you could build a fortune of wealth in the trillions, and if you ignored the amazing grace of Jesus' life, death, and resurrection in your place, you would have successfully gained the whole world and yet forfeited your eternal soul. Please don't give up the eternal for the temporal. Don't cling to that which is eternally worthless while snubbing that which is priceless.

In conclusion, some of you may be asking how my cancer story resolved from 2001. After a minor surgery and another major surgery, I was given a clean bill of health, which lasted for twenty years. I'm thankful for the doctors, the nurses, and the friends and families who prayed for me with my first round of cancer. And though I would never want to go through those surgeries and the mental angst again, I can say that my cancer may have been one of the best things that has ever happened to me because it knocked me flat on my back and helped me to look in the right direction.

Before my cancer in 2001, I was looking to other things for happiness and satisfaction. I learned from C.S. Lewis that God could not give me happiness and peace apart from Himself because soul-satisfying happiness apart from Him does not exist.[52]

Fast forward to April 2021, twenty years after my original diagnosis. My life is full, and I've been cancer-free for twenty years. I am in the throes of running a growing wealth management practice, being a husband to my wife, a dad to two beautiful boys, and writing a book about the four dimensions of financial peace of mind. But I recently got the call from my doctor, "I've got some tough news for you. It's not good." Then, the gut punch.

Yes, friends, on the twentieth anniversary of my original diagnosis, I received a second testicular cancer diagnosis in my abdomen and chest. Same cancer, very rare to get it again twenty years later. Again, Lord, teach us to number our days that we may gain a heart of wisdom. Testicular cancer is generally treatable, but the bad news is, it means three months of intense chemotherapy and probably another major surgery to get rid of it all.

I am literally writing these words to you while being hooked up to a chemo IV in the hospital and thinking about what I would change in this chapter about God's love for us given my current circumstance—I'm nauseous 24/7, all my hair has fallen out, I can't eat because my favorite foods taste like dish soap, and the chemo makes me feel like a shell of a human being. Last week, I sat and blankly stared at a wall without speaking for three days counting down the seconds to when this would be over. I knew chemotherapy was tough, but this has been far worse than I imagined. It is without question the most miserable experience of my life and there is not a close second. It begs the question: When life feels like it is on a downward spiral, does that change the validity of anything we've just talked about regarding Jesus and his love?

No. It does not. After much thought and reflection, I've concluded that nothing written above should change because the Gospel of Jesus is true regardless of my circumstances. I'm once again keenly aware that our life is but a vapor, and none of us are promised tomorrow. It reminds me of an analogy that Randy Alcorn shares in *The Treasure Principle*, where he says that eternity is like a never-ending line, and our time on this earth is represented by a tiny dot on that long line.[53] His admonition to us is to live for the line, not the dot. Which are you living for? Are you investing your life on an eighty-year time

> *"Are you investing your life on an eighty-year time horizon or an eighty-million-year time horizon?"*

Retire to the Fullest

horizon or an eighty-million-year time horizon? Again, what good would it do you to gain the whole world in your eighty years, yet forfeit your soul and live apart from God's goodness for eighty million years?

Are you hoping money will satisfy you? It will not. Are you hoping fame, power, or pleasure will satisfy you? They will not. Are you hoping that being a good person (i.e., religion) will satisfy you? It will not. Only Jesus offers to satisfy you by taking your place, taking your guilt, and replacing it with life to the fullest. That good news, that amazing grace, is why I included this chapter in *Retire to the Fullest*. What better way to engage in your second chapter of life? Friend, my hope and prayer are that you would reject a retirement of withdrawal and enjoy a retirement of being fully alive financially, emotionally, relationally, and spiritually.

Let's Review

- Money, success, fame, and pleasure simply do not satisfy the deepest longings of our hearts.
- If we find ourselves with the desire that nothing in this world can satisfy, the most probable explanation is that we were made for more than this world can offer. (Lewis)
- Jesus claimed that a relationship with God through Him is the only thing that would ever satisfy us completely. Many of us think of Jesus as a nice guy or good teacher, but His claims squarely put Him in the category of liar, lunatic, or Lord. He never intended to simply be known as a nice teacher.
- Religion requires you to "do" something to be accepted, whereas the Gospel declares you accepted once you receive what Jesus has "done" on your behalf. (Greear)
- "Our question should not be how much money I should give, but rather we should humbly ask how much money I should keep." (Cortines/Baumer)
- We have a great exchange where Jesus takes all of our sin and shame and insecurity and replaces those things with His perfection and purity and humble confidence. All that is mine becomes His, and all that is His becomes mine.
- "Christianity preaches the infinite worth of that which is seemingly worthless and the infinite worthlessness of that which is seemingly so valued." (Bonhoeffer)
- You could build a fortune of wealth in the trillions, and if you ignored the amazing grace of Jesus' life, death, and resurrection in your place, you would have successfully gained the whole world and yet forfeited your eternal soul.

APPENDIX

APPENDIX 1

Kinder Questions to Help You Envision and Articulate Your Ideal Second Half

1. Try to imagine you just won a billion dollars in the lottery. Somehow, you managed to become completely financially secure. How would you live your life from here on out? This question helps you determine what matters to you in life.
2. Assume you get a phone call from your doctor to tell you he has some really bad news. You have an incurable illness, and sometime within the next five to ten years, you are going to abruptly pass away. You have five to ten years to live, and the good part in this example is that you're never going to feel sick. You're going to be fully healthy up until the point when you drop dead. But the bad part is that you're not going to get any notice until the moment of your death. You're just going to drop dead with no pain. So the second Kinder question for you is, if you got that phone call, what are you going to do with the five to ten years you have left? And what are you doing currently in your life that you would change in light of that phone call from your doctor? This question helps you prioritize what is most important to you.
3. Pretend with me for a moment that you get another phone call from your doctor, and he shocks you with the news that you have *one day* left to live. What dreams will go unfulfilled? Think about what you wish you had finished or what you wish you had been a part of. This question helps you identify what you would mourn most if your life were cut short, giving you a starting point for goals to set.

APPENDIX 2

Questions to Quantify the Key Variables in Retirement

1. At what age do you want to pivot to another passion? This is the age when you stop drawing an income from your paycheck and draw an income from your investments instead.
2. What are your expenses going to be in retirement? How much does it cost you to live once the mortgage is paid off and the kids are off the payroll? Be sure to include healthcare expenses and potential long-term care costs, especially if your parents need long-term care.
3. Is there a general amount you'd like to leave to heirs?
4. Is there a general amount you'd like to leave to charity?
5. What are all those things you've always wanted to do, and what does it cost to do them?
6. What do you want to spend your time doing in your second half? Think through hobbies, causes, and so forth.

APPENDIX 3

Net Worth Worksheet

Assets	Amount	Liabilities	Amount
Cash:		Mortgage:	
401k/403b:		Line of credit:	
IRAs:		Car loan:	
Nonretirement investments:		Credit card:	
House value:		Other debts:	
Other assets:			
Total assets:		Total liabilities:	

Total assets – Total liabilities = Net Worth

Net Worth Detail - All Resources

This is your Net Worth Detail as of 02/03/2022. Your Net Worth is the difference between what you own (your Assets) and what you owe (your Liabilities). To get an accurate Net Worth statement, make certain all of your Assets and Liabilities are entered.

Description	George	Martha	Joint	Total
Investment Assets				
Employer Retirement Plans				
George 401k	$1,000,000			$1,000,000
Marthas 403b	$2,500,000			$2,500,000
Taxable and/or Tax-Free Accounts				
Cash Equivalent			$150,000	$150,000
George & Martha JTWROS			$1,000,000	$1,000,000
Total Investment Assets:	$3,500,000	$0	$1,150,000	$4,650,000
Other Assets				
Home and Personal Assets				
White House, Pennsylvania Ave			$1,000,000	$1,000,000
Total Other Assets:	$0	$0	$1,000,000	$1,000,000
Liabilities				
Personal Real Estate Loan:				
Mortgage			$100,000	$100,000
Total Liabilities:	$0	$0	$100,000	$100,000
Net Worth:				**$5,550,000**

See Important Disclosure Information section in this Report for explanations of assumptions, limitations, methodologies, and a glossary.

Prepared for : George and Martha Washington   Company: Adams Chetwood Wealth Management   Prepared by: Eric Chetwood

ABOUT THE AUTHOR

Eric Chetwood was born and raised in Winston-Salem, NC. He graduated from the Kenan-Flagler Business School at the University of North Carolina at Chapel Hill in 2003. After graduation, he completed a yearlong biblical scholarship and servant leadership program through Denton Bible Church in Denton, TX. He began his wealth management career the following year in 2004 and completed coursework and successfully passed the Certified Financial Planner® exam in 2007. Eric leads a team that currently manages over $300 million in client assets in Durham, NC. Determined not to just make rich people richer, he strives to guide clients to financial peace of mind by caring for them in every way that money impacts them: financially, emotionally, relationally, and spiritually.

Away from the office, Eric serves as a directional Elder at the Summit Church in Durham, NC, and as a board member for the NC Study Center at UNC-CH. He and his wife, Allison, have two incredible sons and are passionate about adoption advocacy, microfinance, and social businesses. Some of Eric's favorite things are traveling with Allison, coaching his boys' sports teams, and enjoying great meals with friends. To connect with Eric, visit www.retiretothefullest.com

ENDNOTES

Introduction
1. Andy Stanley, *Principal of the Path: How to Get from Where You Are to Where You Want to Be* (Nashville: Thomas Nelson, 2008).

Chapter 1
2. https://www.brainyquote.com/quotes/benjamin_franklin_138217.
3. George Kinder: Financial Life Planning and His Three Questions, May 30, 2019; https://www.youtube.com/watch?v=FEncdAA6X5M.
4. Psalm 90:12, *Holy Bible, New International Version,* NIV Copyright 1973, 1978, 1984, 2011 by Biblica, Inc. Used by permission. All rights reserved worldwide.

Chapter 3
5. Emmie Martin, "Warren Buffet recommends a simple exercise before you buy any stock: write down your why"; CNBC.com; updated Monday, November 23, 2020. https://www.cnbc.com/2020/02/24/warren-buffett-dont-buy-stocks-because-you-think-they-will-perform.html.
6. Farrelly, Bobby, and Peter Farrelly. 1994. Dumb and Dumber. United States: New Line Cinema.

Chapter 4
7. Harry Markowitz, "Harry Markowitz's Modern Portfolio Theory: The Efficient Frontier," The Guided Choice; https://www.guidedchoice.com/video/dr-harry-markowitz-father-of-modern-portfolio-theory/.

8   2021 CFA Level 1 Exam: CFA Study Preparation, Subject 5: Portfolio Risk; https://analystnotes.com/cfa-study-notes-portfolio-risk.html.

Chapter 5

9   Nick Murray, *Simple Wealth, Inevitable Wealth,* pp. 86–90.

10 Source: Wolfe Research. Only companies with market cap of at least $250 million included.

Chapter 6

11 Nick Murray, *Simple Wealth, Inevitable Wealth: How You and Your Financial Advisor Can Grow Your Fortune in Stock Mutual Funds* (The Nick Murray Company, 1999), 23.

12 LymeLine.com: Community News for Lyme and Old Lyme, CT; Reading Uncertainly? 'Misbehaving: The Making of Behavioral Economics' by Richard Thaler, a book review by Felix Kloman, January 7, 2017; https://lymeline.com/2017/01/reading-uncertainly-misbehaving-the-making-of-behavioral-economics-by-richard-thaler/.

13 Opinion: Warren E. Buffett, "Buy American. I am." The New York Times, October 16, 2008. https://www.nytimes.com/2008/10/17/opinion/17buffett.html.

14 Davis Advisors, Wisdom of Great Investors - Peter Lynch; https://www.davisadvisors.com/davissma/wisdom.

15 Murray, *Simple Wealth, Inevitable Wealth,* 33–34.

16 Murray, *Simple Wealth, Inevitable Wealth,* 23.

17 Murray, *Simple Wealth, Inevitable Wealth,* 12.

Chapter 7

18 The Princess Diaries. [United States] : Burbank, Calif. :Walt Disney Home Entertainment, 2001; Distributed by Buena Vista Home Entertainment, 20042001. Directed by Garry Marshall, et al.

19 Dhaval Dave, Inas Rashad, and Jasmina Spasojevic. "The Effects of Retirement on Physical and Mental Health Outcomes," National Bureau Of Economic Research, (Cambridge, MA, March 2006). http://www.nber.org/papers/w12123.

20 Bob Buford, *Halftime: Moving from Success to Significance* (Grand Rapids: Zondervan, 2016).

21. Bob Buford, *Halftime: Moving from Success to Significance* (Grand Rapids: Zondervan, 2016), 139.
22. Alex A., The Vintage News, "Alfred Nobel created the Nobel Prize as a false obituary declared him 'The Merchant of Death'; October 14, 2016. https://www.thevintagenews.com/2016/10/14/alfred-nobel-created-the-nobel-prize-as-a-false-obituary-declared-him-the-merchant-of-death/.
23. Lara Casey, Cultivate Your Life Podcast, Episode 24, "You Know All Those Things?" https://laracasey.com/cultivate-your-life-podcast-episode-024-you-know-all-those-things/.
24. de Witt, Lorna, Lori Campbell, Jenny Ploeg, Candace L. Kemp, and Carolyn Rosenthal. "You're Saying Something by Giving Things to Them:' Communication and Family Inheritance." European Journal of Ageing 10, no. 3 (2013): 181–89. https://doi.org/10.1007/s10433-013-0262-z.
25. Maggie Germano, "Despite Their Priorities, Nearly Half Of Americans over 55 Still Don't Have A Will," Forbes.com, February 15, 2019; https://www.forbes.com/sites/maggiegermano/2019/02/15/despite-their-priorities-nearly-half-of-americans-over-55-still-dont-have-a-will/?sh=6486e7005238.
26. "Half of America Sees Estate Planning as Tool of the Ultra-Rich"; WealthCounsel, October 16, 2016. https://www.prnewswire.com/news-releases/half-of-america-sees-estate-planning-as-tool-of-the-ultra-rich-300346690.html.
27. *Ryznar, Margaret; Devaux, Angelique (2014). "Au Revoir, Will Contests: Comparative Lessons for Preventing Will Contests." Nevada Law Journal.* **14** *(1): 1. Retrieved 6 September 2017.*
28. Note: "The lower a person's annual income falls below that benchmark, the unhappier he or she feels. But no matter how much more than $75,000 people make, they don't report any greater degree of happiness," Time reported in 2010, citing a study from Princeton University conducted by economist Angus Deaton and psychologist Daniel Kahneman; https://www.cnbc.com/2017/11/20/how-much-money-you-need-to-be-happy-according-to-wealth-experts.html.

Chapter 8

29 https://en.wikipedia.org/wiki/Water_stagnation; Note 3: Ling, Fangqiong; Whitaker, Rachel; LeChevallier, Mark W.; Liu, Wen-Tso (1 June 2018). "Drinking water microbiome assembly induced by water stagnation". The ISME Journal. 12 (6): 1520–1531. doi:10.1038/s41396-018-0101-5. ISSN 1751-7362. PMC 5955952. PMID 29588495.

30 Andy Stanley, *How to Be Rich: It's Not What You Have, It's What You Do With What You Have* (Grand Rapids: Zondervan, 2014), 31.

31 Stanley, *How to Be Rich*, 43.

32 Stanley, *How to Be Rich*, 35.

33 Elijah Davidson, *God and Money: What Does the Bible Say about Money and Wealth?* (Independently published by Create Space, 2014), 83.

34 Christian Smith and Hilary Davidson, "Science of Generosity Project," University of Notre Dame, "The Paradox of Generosity." Elijah Davidson, *God and Money: What Does the Bible Say about Money and Wealth?* (Independently published by Create Space, 2014), pp. 83–84.

Chapter 9

35 Matthew 16:26, Holy Bible, New International Version®, NIV® Copyright ©1973, 1978, 1984, 2011 by Biblica, Inc.® Used by permission. All rights reserved worldwide.

36 Ecclesiastes 2:10–11, Holy Bible, New International Version®, NIV® Copyright ©1973, 1978, 1984, 2011 by Biblica, Inc.® Used by permission. All rights reserved worldwide.

37 60 Minutes: Steve Kroft interview with Tom Brady on winning, 2005: There's "got to be more than this." https://www.youtube.com/watch?v=-TA4_fVkv3c.

38 Corinne Heller, " Lady Gaga Says Nothing Is More "Isolating" Than Being Famous: How Her Attitude About Fame Has Evolved, E-Online, June 3, 2016, https://www.eonline.com/news/770079/lady-gaga-says-nothing-is-more-isolating-than-being-famous-how-her-attitude-about-fame-has-evolved.

39 Van Morrison, https://quotefancy.com/quote/1334759/Van-Morrison-Being-famous-was-extremely-disappointing-for-me-When-I-became-famous-it-was.

40 Jesse Eisenberg, https://whatsmyquote.com/quote/the-only-way-to-be-turned-off-to-being-famous-is-to-be-famous
41 Jim Carrey, https://quotesupdate.com/jim-carrey-quotes/.
42 C.S. Lewis, *Mere Christianity* (New York City: HarperCollins Publishing, 1952). Also, https://www.goodreads.com/quotes/462154-the-christian-says-creatures-are-not-born-with-desires-unless.
43 *Mere Christianity* by C.S. Lewis @ copyright 1942, 1943, 1944, 1952 CS Lewis Pte Ltd. Extract used with permission
44 J.D. Greear, "Gospel Above All," blog post (March 12, 2018) https://jdgreear.com/gospel-above-all/.
45 Matthew 6:19–21, *New American Standard Bible*®, Copyright © 1960, 1971, 1977, 1995 by The Lockman Foundation. All rights reserved.
46 Davidson, *God and Money: What Does the Bible Say about Money and Wealth?* (Independently published by Create Space, 2014), 62.
47 Randy Alcorn, *The Treasure Principle: Unlocking the Secret of Joyful Giving* (Colorado Springs: Multnomah Books, 2001).
48 2 Corinthians 8:9, *Holy Bible, New International Version*®, NIV® Copyright ©1973, 1978, 1984, 2011 by Biblica, Inc.® Used by permission. All rights reserved worldwide.
49 Romans 8:1, *Holy Bible, New International Version*®, NIV® Copyright ©1973, 1978, 1984, 2011 by Biblica, Inc.® Used by permission. All rights reserved worldwide.
50 Timothy Keller, https://timothykeller.com.
51 Dietrich Bonhoeffer, https://quotefancy.com/quote/794726/Dietrich-Bonhoeffer-Christianity-preaches-the-infinite-worth-of-that-which-is-seemingly.
52 C.S. Lewis, https://www.brainyquote.com/quotes/c_s_lewis_151474.
53 Randy Alcorn, *The Treasure Principle: Unlocking the Secret of Joyful Giving* (Colorado Springs: Multnomah Books, 2001).

CPSIA information can be obtained
at www.ICGtesting.com
Printed in the USA
BVHW031125260423
663000BV00002B/280